theatr

D0531095

Theatre&
Series Standing Order: ISBN 978–0–230–20327–3 paperback

You can receive further titles in this series as they are published by placing a standing order. Please contact your bookseller or, in the case of difficulty, write to us at the address below with your name and address, the title of the series, and the ISBN quoted above.

Customer Services Department, Palgrave Macmillan Ltd.
Houndmills, Basingstoke, Hampshire, RG21 6XS, England

theatre & feeling

Erin Hurley

palgrave
macmillan

First published 2010 by
PALGRAVE MACMILLAN

Palgrave Macmillan in the UK is an imprint of Macmillan Publishers Limited, registered in England, company number 785998, of Houndmills, Basingstoke, Hampshire RG21 6XS.

Palgrave Macmillan in the US is a division of St Martin's Press LLC, 175 Fifth Avenue, New York, NY 10010.

Palgrave Macmillan is the global academic imprint of the above companies and has companies and representatives throughout the world.

Palgrave® and Macmillan® are registered trademarks in the United States, the United Kingdom, Europe and other countries.

ISBN 978-0-230-21846-8   paperback

This book is printed on paper suitable for recycling and made from fully managed and sustained forest sources. Logging, pulping and manufacturing processes are expected to conform to the environmental regulations of the country of origin.

A catalogue record for this book is available from the British Library.

A catalog record for this book is available from the Library of Congress.

10 9 8 7 6 5
19 18 17 16 15 14

Printed and bound in China

contents

series editors' preface

The theatre is everywhere, from entertainment districts to the fringes, from the rituals of government to the ceremony of the courtroom, from the spectacle of the sporting arena to the theatres of war. Across these many forms stretches a theatrical continuum through which cultures both assert and question themselves.

Theatre has been around for thousands of years, and the ways we study it have changed decisively. It's no longer enough to limit our attention to the canon of Western dramatic literature. Theatre has taken its place within a broad spectrum of performance, connecting it with the wider forces of ritual and revolt that thread through so many spheres of human culture. In turn, this has helped make connections across disciplines; over the past fifty years, theatre and performance have been deployed as key metaphors and practices with which to rethink gender, economics, war, language, the fine arts, culture and one's sense of self.

Theatre & is a long series of short books which hopes to capture the restless interdisciplinary energy of theatre and performance. Each book explores connections between theatre and some aspect of the wider world, asking how the theatre might illuminate the world and how the world might illuminate the theatre. Each book is written by a leading theatre scholar and represents the cutting edge of critical thinking in the discipline.

We have been mindful, however, that the philosophical and theoretical complexity of much contemporary academic writing can act as a barrier to a wider readership. A key aim for these books is that they should all be readable in one sitting by anyone with a curiosity about the subject. The books are challenging, pugnacious, visionary sometimes and, above all, clear. We hope you enjoy them.

Jen Harvie and Dan Rebellato

foreword

My dedication to a life in the theatre is unequivocally related to emotion, feeling, and sensation, and I suspect I share this 'secret cause' with many others in the profession, on both sides of the footlights. And yet emotion and feeling is rarely the subject of our discussions or analysis. Why do we discuss feeling in the theatre so rarely? Perhaps we shy away because the subject is too dangerous. We are in the business of creating experiences for audiences but we know that feelings and emotions can be easily misused, manipulated, and abused.

I cry easily. In a film a boy runs across a field towards his missing dog and I weep. I burst into tears at advertisements. I get goose bumps from a high-jump feat. It is easy in the theatre to create a moment on stage when everyone in the audience feels the same thing. But what I find much more interesting and challenging is to stage a moment in which everyone has different associations and feels something different.

I cringe if I hear an actor say, 'If I feel it, they will feel it.' The notion that the actor and the audience feel the same sensations at the same moment leads to a solipsistic approach to acting and easy dismissal on the part of the audience. A scholar sitting in on a run-through of a one-woman show I directed entitled *Room*, based upon the writings of Virginia Woolf, was overcome with emotion at a particular point in the play. Later he interviewed Ellen Lauren, the actress, and asked her what she had been thinking about during this specific section of the play. Ellen responded, 'I was counting.' Owing to the intricate choreography and precise musical cues in the scene, Ellen found it necessary to count. The scholar was appalled. He could not believe that what had swept him away so thoroughly was a section in which the actor was counting. But, in fact, the actor was busy, engaged in setting up the necessary conditions for the audience to respond.

Despite the fact that we theatre people share an intense interest and curiosity in the subject of feeling, I nonetheless avoid analysing the subject directly in the process of a rehearsal. The issue is slippery and complicated and easily misunderstood. The worst way to approach feeling with actors is directly; rather, feeling is a byproduct of a precise arrangement of circumstances. A person interested in the phenomenon of a solar eclipse does not look directly at the sun, which is far too dangerous for the eyes. She or he gazes to the side or looks at the reflection upon a piece of cardboard in order to experience the sun's eclipse. But the point of the sideways gaze is not the cardboard; rather, it is the interest in the sun. In a similar sense, in a rehearsal, instead of discussing feeling, I tend to concentrate on precise details and technical points, not because I am so fascinated by these issues but rather because I am attempting to set up the circumstances in which feeling can occur. I do not try to control the uncontrollable or to manipulate feeling or emotion to occur at a particular moment. Attempting to manufacture emotion and feeling directly can lead to facile theatre and an experience that is forgotten upon its conclusion. Complex and memorable feelings in the theatre are a glorious byproduct of a very precise work on form, psychology, and timing.

To be in the presence of actors is a constant thrill to me. Actors are required to be incredibly alive and sensitive to the slight variations in the environment and to the vicissitudes, moods, signals, and minute alterations of those around them. To be in the room with humans functioning at this highest level of wakefulness, awareness, and courageousness is both sexy and thrilling. I experience a contact high from these extraordinary beings. To be in the presence of someone who is actually noticing, not faking or feigning, but truly noticing, is a remarkable occasion. As Martha Graham often said, 'The body does not lie.' An actor noticing a beeper going off in the back of the theatre or responding to a fellow actor's sudden change in tempo, all the while maintaining the forward momentum of the play, engages the audience in this very balancing act on a moment-to-moment basis. In the instant that we all are sharing, the actors and the audience, this responsiveness is real and visceral and can change the temperature of a room full of observers.

Erin Hurley in *Theatre & Feeling* proposes astute and useful ways of examining feeling in the theatre. She starts by breaking down feeling into affect, emotion, and mood. What I described just now, the thrill of being in the presence of actors who are radiantly experiencing the present moment, falls under affect. Affect means 'feeling associated with action'. Our blood rushes faster, our mirror neurons spike new synaptic activity throughout our bodies, adrenalin courses throughout the system, and, as an added bonus, we are literally massaged by the actor's voice. This visceral experience, one of the leading attributes of all encounters with art, is a large part of why we bother to engage with art in the first place. The increased adrenalin resulting from the experience sharpens the mind and focuses the attention.

Israeli psychologist Daniel Kahneman proposes that we can think of ourselves as two separate beings. He distinguishes between the experiencing self and the remembering self. The experiencing self lives in the present moment. The remembering self keeps score and creates stories from the experiences of the experiencing self. What we keep from our experiences becomes story. According to Kahneman, there is a difference between the experience and the memory of the experience. We go to the theatre for the direct visceral experience but also for the anticipated memories.

Hurley differentiates emotion from affect by the presence of memory. The mind interprets immediate experience via memories in the form of expectations, previous experience, and cultural assumptions. This act of interpretation leads an individual or an audience member to create associations, meaning, and conclusions. New memories are added to existing ones. What creates memory? Experience and sensation become memory via emotion. The more emotion that is generated in the heat of the experience, the more likely the memory is to 'stick'. Emotion seals memory. The stronger the emotion, the more accessible is the memory. It is my hope to make theatre that is both visceral and exciting in the moment (affective) but that also creates pathways to new and lasting memories.

It turns out that memory is actually a protein that is formed in the heat of experience. If you think back on formative experiences that you have had in your life, the ones that are accessible are memories formed in the presence of emotion. For me, my initial experience in the theatre at the age of fifteen was a highly emotional encounter with what was both unfamiliar and magnetically attractive. This experience led me to choose the theatre as a profession. I can remember this experience easily. To access a memory, a particular synaptic path must be created that leads to this protein.

Mood is the third kind of feeling that Hurley explores. In the theatre I understand mood as the underlying context in which an individual or a group experiences the play. Music or rhythmic movement that inclines audiences towards certain kinds of emotional responses and reactions can aid the mood of both individuals and a group. A sound design can be a great mood enhancer, as can a dance break or a procession across the stage. Jean-Jacques Lemaître, the music director of Théâtre du Soleil, once remarked, 'Music makes theatre bearable.' From my experience, this can work for or against a production. Music is a powerful mood inducer and can too easily overwhelm a production and become a cheap ruse towards emotion.

Hurley proposes that theatre might well be defined as 'a realm of active emotion'.

I concur. I initially chose the theatre because it grabbed me by the collar, thrilled me, confused me, and then tossed me into a swirl of unfamiliarity, proposing by example that the scope of life can be far wider and wilder than ever I imagined. This magnetic forceful affect is the draw for theatre-makers and audiences alike. We are attracted by the sweep of feeling, of emotion, of adrenaline, surges of dopamine and serotonin, and new neural pathways forged in the brain and extending throughout the entire body. We crave the feelings engendered in the experience of the theatre. For me, the process of rehearsal as well as performance is life heated up, intensified, and put under a microscope. The emotional highs and lows of a two-hour play happen more quickly than in daily life because the repertoire of feeling is compressed into a smaller amount of space and time. But the pathway to such feeling is not so simple. Only if all the circumstances are lined up in the correct way is the unexpected possible.

Balancing the thrill of affect, the complexities of emotion, and the right mood is difficult but necessary in the practice of making effectual theatre. The process begins with the artist's conscious responsibility towards the audience's experience and journey. Despite my hesitation to overanalyse feeling in the theatre, I find Hurley's book valuable and useful. Reading *Theatre & Feeling* can help us to make our choices with more consciousness and accountability.

Anne Bogart is the Artistic Director of the SITI Company, which she founded with Japanese director Tadashi Suzuki in 1992. She is a professor at Columbia University, where she runs the Graduate Directing Program. Works with SITI include Antigone; Under Construction; Freshwater; Who Do You Think You Are; Radio Macbeth; Hotel Cassiopeia; Death and the Ploughman; La Dispute; Score; bobrauschenbergamerica; Room; War of the Worlds; Cabin Pressure; The Radio Play; Alice's Adventures; Culture of Desire; Bob; Going, Going, Gone; Small Lives/Big Dreams; The Medium; *Noel Coward's* Hay Fever *and* Private Lives; *August Strindberg's* Miss Julie; *and Charles Mee's* Orestes. *She is the author of three books:* A Director Prepares, The Viewpoints Book, *and* And Then, You Act.

theatre & feeling

Beloved theatre

When one asks theatre people – actors, scenographers, scholars – why they do what they do, the response is often some variation on the theme of love. They'll say they do theatre 'because I *had* to' or 'because I couldn't imagine *not* doing theatre' or, simply, 'because I love the theatre'. Theatrical biographies and autobiographies whose titles equate the actor's very life to the theatre – such as *Theatre in My Blood: A Biography of John Cranko* by John Percival (1983) or Moss Hart's *Act One: An Autobiography* (1989) – reinforce this impression. Western theatre's earliest theorist, Aristotle, maintains that imitation (or mimesis) is a primary and universal human pleasure. What is true for theatre artists appears to be true for theatre-goers as well. Recent data indicate that a significant number of people attend the theatre for its emotional pay-off. In a 2005 national survey in the United States that Susan Bennett quotes in her 2006 article 'Theatre Audiences, Redux', 56.5 per cent of respondents said that their 'major motivation' for attending a cultural event was the 'emotionally rewarding' experience it offered. As significant, another report on arts participation quoted by Bennett found that three-quarters of the arts events people attend are amateur productions; in other words, they are events put on by those whose artistic practice is founded, by definition, in love (the French *amateur* literally means 'lover'). For artists and spectators, scholars and students, professionals and amateurs, theatre is a passion. It moves us. *Theatre & Feeling* takes this commonplace seriously.

Questions of feeling have always been central to theatre, from the Greek philosopher Aristotle's identification of catharsis as the central aim of tragedy in his *Poetics* (fifth century BCE) to the twentieth-century German playwright, director, and theorist Bertolt Brecht's technique of interleaving emotional response with rational or analytical response in his Epic theatre. Feeling runs like a red thread through the history of theatrical production – east and west, north and south. Among those who have treated this topic are the ancient Indian sage Bharata, to whom the primary theatrical treatise of classical Indian theatre and dance, *Natya Sastra*, is attributed; Hildegard von Bingen, in her devotional plays of the Middle Ages; eighteenth-century English dramatic critics and newspapermen Joseph Addison and Richard Steele; and Augusto Boal, the twentieth-century Brazilian activist playwright and pedagogue. Critics have asked how and at what level performance engages spectators' emotions. For example, how do expressive cues such as music and lighting set a mood or convey an emotional tone for an audience? Scholars have inquired into the connection between form and feeling. How does a tragedy arouse pity and fear? What makes melodrama so consistently affecting, even if we say we despise its hackneyed plots and find its stereotyped characters laughable? Acting teachers, theorists, and practitioners have sought to understand the relationship between human emotions and their display. Since at least the seventeenth century, actors have asked themselves whether they need to feel the same emotions as their character to convey them convincingly to the audience. How can they summon 'real' or 'authentic' emotion *repeatedly* in performance?

This book brings theatrical feeling into focus as a research object and method in theatre studies. It traces the main preoccupations of dramatic theory relating to emotion in a way that will equip students with a guide to theatre's emotional effects and establish a baseline for further research in this rich and emergent area of inquiry. Along the way, I'll investigate the purposes of theatrical emotion. Should it contribute to a moral or pedagogical programme? Is it there to make us feel more alive? We'll reflect on 'feel-good' and 'feel-bad' forms of theatre such as the mid-twentieth-century American musical and classical Greek tragedy, respectively. The 'feel-ambivalent' theatre of Chekhov will play a clarifying role in the book's final section, in which I analyse the precepts of twentieth-century Stanislavskian acting theory. There, we'll approach from multiple perspectives the perennial question of how actors communicate an internal emotional life to an audience.

What this tour through dramatic theory and theatre history will show is the centrality – or, more strongly, the necessity – of feeling to theatre. In the sections that follow, you'll come to see that feeling and theatre are fundamentally linked. I make this argument by demonstrating first how feeling provides theatre's *raison d'être*. Excursuses into theatrical form and into the neuroscience of spectatorship allow me to conclude that doing things with feeling is the primary reason for theatre's existence. Furthermore, feeling carries theatre's communicated meanings and informs its significance to theatre-goers. In this way, theatre's solicitation, management, and display of feelings – what I will call its 'feeling-labour' – is the most important aspect of theatre's cultural work. It is what finally makes theatre matter.

Theatre and feeling

So to begin, let's think about this conjunction between theatre and feeling. What is its nature? And why does it merit our attention? On the one hand, as my opening pages have suggested, the answer to these questions is obvious. Theatre traffics frequently and fundamentally in feeling in all its forms – affect, sensation, emotion, mood – which I'll detail below. Indeed, theatre might best be defined as a realm of active emotion. In his *Dramatic Technique* (1919), a book that outlines the precepts of dramaturgy (or how plays are constructed), George Pierce Baker defined a play as 'the shortest distance from emotions to emotions' (p. 21). In his 1938 collection of essays, translated into English in a 1958 Grove Press edition, *The Theatre and Its Double*, Antonin Artaud pronounced, 'The actor is an athlete of the heart' (p. 133). And according to M. H. Abrams's landmark work in literary criticism *The Mirror and the Lamp* (1953), since at least the Romantics of the late eighteenth and early nineteenth centuries, the purpose of all forms of art, and of theatre in particular, has been to express emotion, that is, to project it to the external world from its 'natural' interior location by means of expressive signs such as gesture or vocal intonation or painterly attack. More anecdotally, you may have the impression that theatre people, scholars, and audiences already talk about feeling and in a language of feeling all the time. You would be correct, of course. Much of our common theatrical vocabulary – especially those words and concepts used to describe and evaluate the experience of going to the theatre – is an emotional one. Many of our discipline's keywords are drawn from the lexicon of feeling: catharsis, empathy, sense memory, dramatic tension, a rave review, and so on.

On the other hand, despite the common invocation of feeling across time periods and genres of performance, and despite the frequency with which feeling enters our discussions of the theatre, the match between theatre and feeling is also rather peculiar. Consider first the extraordinary intensity of the feelings generated by theatrical performance. I'm thinking here not only of being profoundly moved by, say, Willy Loman's suicide at the end of

Death of a Salesman (Morosco Theatre, New York, 1949), when he calculates that the value to his family of his life-insurance policy exceeds that of his life; I'm mindful too of the outsize emotional engagements among, for example, musical theatre aficionados debating the relative merits of a mid-century American musical such as *Gypsy* (Broadway Theatre, New York, 1959) and a contemporary musical such as *Rent* (Nederlander Theatre, New York, 1996). Part of the dream of making a life in the theatre lies in the grand emotional experiences the profession offers; that joke about actors constantly falling in love with their co-stars is but one symptom of the heightened emotional register at which theatre people often work. Québécois actress, director, and writer Pol Pelletier writes lovingly of the hothouse environment of collective creation – in which a group of people work collectively to devise a show – in her solo performance *Joie* [Joy], performed at different Montreal locations between 1990 and 1993 and now translated into English by Linda Gaboriau in Louise H. Forsyth's 2008 *Anthology of Québec Women's Plays in English Translation, Volume 2 (1987–2003)*:

> Collective creation is exhausting. You spend three to five months with the same group of people, five or six days a week, eight hours a day. ... Every day, since you couldn't hide behind a script, a director, a role, you had to expose yourself – who you were, what you believed, what you loved, what you wanted. And that

meant you related to the others, really, truly, brutally sometimes. (p. 143)

In her description of the intensity of collective creation, Pelletier highlights the emotional forces that can be released through the really, truly brutal relationship between actors within the fictional circumstances of theatrical production. Theatre is bigger than life precisely because its emotional repertoire is bigger than our quotidian one; although it is not uncommon for two hours' traffic on the stage to take a character from being a contented king to an ashamed exile, those emotional highs and lows are not generally experienced offstage at such close intervals or at such extremes.

As further evidence of the odd conjunction of theatre and feeling, we might wonder at the strangeness of having *real* emotional responses to what are usually *unreal* (that is, fictional) situations and characters onstage. Why and how does Arthur Miller's tragedy for the common man move audiences despite their knowledge of the story and its outcome? *Death of a Salesman* is an American theatre classic, after all, that is frequently performed on regional theatre circuits and regularly mined for actors' audition pieces. And how does it overcome the fact that 'Willy' does not exist in the real world? He is, rather, portrayed by an actor reciting lines Miller wrote more than sixty years ago.

So they're a funny pair, theatre and feeling – a match at once seemingly natural and yet not so obvious as it may at first appear. It is, I think, precisely this combination of their at-once over-easy coincidence and their not particularly evident relation that makes feeling so fundamental to theatre. As Nicholas Ridout contends in his 2007 book on affect in theatrical reception, *Stage Fright, Animals and Other Theatrical Problems*, theatre is an affect machine – both by design and, most provocatively for Ridout, by mistake. In terms of design, over the past two millennia, theatre professionals have developed an arsenal of theatrical effects to display, create, and incite feeling in the theatre, effects that would overcome or mask the ways in which theatre and feeling do not go together. Perhaps most obviously, actors train to conjure convincing emotions on stage. But the whole gamut of theatre professionals engage in some level of emotional analysis and calibration. Lighting designers create 'warm' and 'cool' stage-washes, descriptors that indicate not only the lighting's colour palette but also its emotional resonance. Sound designers and theatrical musicians likewise strive to convey mood. Each of these categories of theatre artist is attuned to the emotional patterning of the theatrical experience. Thus, music in minor keys encourages feelings of sadness, and the rapid scenic transformations of the nineteenth-century popular stage were meant to be thrilling.

Ridout's thesis points to the curiously perfect match of theatre and feeling; he maintains that theatre can't help but make us feel, even when it doesn't mean to, when it isn't particularly trying to, or when its design fails outright (as in the case of actors breaking up with laughter or experiencing paralysing stage fright). He traces theatre's inevitable affective impact to the circumstances in which theatre happens.

In short, he argues that because we as audience members are aware that the actors onstage are, in fact, at work – and at work for us, while we leisure at the theatre – we become disquieted by our position as consumers of others' labour. Thus the doubled space of theatre – a place of leisure for the audience, a place of labour for the artists and technicians – produces shame, embarrassment, and fear, as well as pleasure, as a matter of course. I concur with Ridout's assessment of those moments of heated intersubjectivity occasioned by the encounter with theatrical production. I would add to his analysis of theatrical labour as *waged* work the idea of theatrical labour as '*feeling*-work' – again, by design and by default.

In my use of 'feeling-work' and 'feeling-labour', I follow the definitions of feminist sociologist Arlie Hochschild in her foundational text *The Managed Heart: Commercialization of Human Feeling* ([1983] 2003), which elaborates a theory of 'emotional labour'. By 'feeling-labour' I intend to capture the work theatre does in making, managing, and moving feeling in all its types (affect, emotions, moods, sensations) in a publicly observable display that is sold to an audience for a wage. I contend that it is theatre's feeling-labours – the display of larger-than-life emotions, the management of our sensate body, and the distribution of affect between stage and auditorium – that draw us in, compel us to return, and most capture our imagination. As such, in addition to being theatre's reason for being, feeling is what is most consequential about theatre. Feeling draws us into the symbolic universe of the theatrical performance by connecting us emotionally with its characters – we might identify with the hero or feel anger towards the villain – and hooking us with its moving narrative structure. In *Utopia in Performance: Finding Hope at the Theater* (2005), Jill Dolan theorises how spectator feeling at the theatre can produce unanticipated alliances, shared pleasures, identifications, and dis-identifications among participants. In this way, theatre's emotional labour also performs social work; by this I mean that via emotional labour, theatre intervenes in how we as a society come to understand ourselves, our values, and our social world.

This is not to say that theatre is not also a place of cognition, of deliberation, of decision. It is that too, of course. Yet it is feeling, not the instruction or reflection theatre provides or occasions, that makes theatre so vital, even necessary, to so many. In what follows, I sketch the philosophical bases for the centrality of feeling to theatre through readings in dramatic theory and cognitive science, and then outline the functional reasons for the necessity of feeling to theatre by looking at dramatic form, the production of meaning in the theatre, and feeling's professional significance to actors in particular. But first, some definitions.

Types of feeling

I must begin this section defining types of feeling by acknowledging that not everyone will be convinced of the value of separating out affect from mood from emotion (particularly the first from the last), most out of a belief in their co-extension. It is a task made complex by the volume of literature on the topic of feeling from disciplines across the humanities, social sciences, and life sciences (especially literary studies, psychology and anthropology, and neuroscience) and by the variation of the terminology across and within these domains of research. My definitional task is further complicated by the fact that the social and theatrical languages of feeling with which theatre people work vary historically and culturally. In personal correspondence, Sara Warner reminded me, for instance, that Aristotle and Bharata compiled rather different lists of primary emotions. I offer the following taxonomy of feeling nonetheless because the ways in which categories of feeling have been differentiated affects how theatre and its emotional labours have come to matter, to be valued (or devalued, as the case may be), and to have a social impact. They inform how theatre works (on us): as noted above and as we will see below, the theatre has developed a range of mechanisms and effects specifically aimed at provoking different categories of feeling, notably affect, emotion, and mood. Moreover, theatre's strong association with sensational feeling has often raised the hackles of philosophers, moralists, and politicians who would prefer theatre's cultural work to be more 'elevated'. This association underpins what Jonas Barish called 'the anti-theatrical prejudice', in a 1981 book of the same name; this is a hostile and censorious attitude towards theatrical entertainments that Barish traces from antiquity to the present day.

Affect

Two men balance on a high wire approximately twelve metres above the bare stage floor. One crouches down holding a long balance pole horizontally and bends his head to his knees, initiating a game of leapfrog. The second takes three quick steps towards his partner and leaps over his crouched form. He loses his footing upon landing – actually, it appears as though he never gains his footing – and careens wildly over the side of the wire, grasping it with one hand only at the last minute. The assembled spectators gasp and hold their breath; our hearts race, our pupils dilate, and goose pimples rise around the circus tent. As the jumper holds on for dear life, swaying back and forth, the audience's focus narrows to the point where the aerialist's hand holds the now undulating wire while his partner also struggles to maintain his precarious balance. After what feels like a very long time, the jumper pulls himself back up onto the high wire and consults with the other aerialist; we in the audience exhale and giggle uncomfortably. Then the performers restart the game of leapfrog. This second time they complete the feat successfully and are rewarded with the spontaneous, thunderous standing ovation of a rapt crowd.

This moment is from the Cirque du Soleil's 2007 show called *KOOZÄ*, which opened in the Cirque du Soleil's distinctive blue-and-yellow *grand chapiteau* (big top) pitched at Montreal's Vieux Port. However, this pattern of tension and release generated by performers and experienced by audiences is not unique to the Cirque du Soleil, nor to this show in particular. Indeed, such thrills are among the building blocks of circus performance and, for many, the reason they might wish to attend the circus or even to 'run away' with it. Moreover, thrills and the responses they engender are fundamental elements of many other kinds of theatrical performance. The kind of heightened awareness they provoke motivated the 'transformation scene' of eighteenth-century pantomime and the 'sensation scene' of nineteenth-century melodrama. But thrills are just the tip of the iceberg when it comes to theatre and feeling. Thrill experiences such as the one I describe above are the most physiologically basic of a repertoire of responses to our environment that are captured under the general rubric of 'feeling'. Scholars tend to call this immediate, uncontrollable, skin-level registration of a change to our environment 'affect'. Affect makes itself known through autonomic reactions, such as sexual arousal or sweating; thus, affects are sets of muscular and/or glandular responses. (The autonomic nervous system helps bodies adapt to changes in their environment; active at all times, it regulates automatic, compensatory reactions – such as pupils dilating when we are thrust into sudden darkness or the adrenal medulla excreting increased amounts of adrenaline to sharpen our concentration in response to threatening circumstances.)

As anyone who has felt a blush steal over her face at the most inopportune time knows, these are responses we cannot consciously control. This is why the great nineteenth-century Italian actress Eleanora Duse's famous onstage, in-character blush when meeting an old lover during a London performance of Hermann Sudermann's *Heimat* in 1895 remains a touchstone of 'true' and absolutely believable acting to this day. George Bernard Shaw wrote that

Duse's character, Magda,

> evidently felt that she had got it safely over and
> might allow herself to think at her ease, and to
> look at him to see how much he had altered.
> Then a terrible thing happened to her. She began
> to blush; and in another moment she was con-
> scious of it, and the blush was slowly spreading
> and deepening until, after a few vain efforts to
> avert her face or to obstruct his view of it without
> seeming to do so, she gave up and hid the blush in
> her hands. After that feat of acting I did not need
> to be told why Duse does not paint an inch thick.
> I could detect no trick in it: it seemed to me a
> perfectly genuine effect of the dramatic imagin-
> ation. (*Our Theatres in the Nineties*, 1931, p. 162)

Affect is unruly that way; it exceeds us by happening against
our will. It is also arguably a common level of human
response. Paul Ekman – whose cross-cultural research
into facial expression, body language, and deceit from an
evolutionary psychology perspective has recently been
popularised in the Fox television series *Lie to Me* – asserts
that each kind of affective response (such as surprise or
disgust) results in a distinctive pan-cultural signal that is
innate and universal to the human species. For example,
data from his experiments over the past forty years sug-
gest that fear is expressed on the human face by raised and
knitted eyebrows, raised upper eyelids, still lower lids, and

horizontally stretched lips ('Expression and the Nature of Emotion', 1984, p. 325). Ekman concludes that these affective expressions are common to all humans because of the human organism's common physiology: our bodies respond in similar patterns because we share the same biological properties.

According to this line of thinking, those universal expressions can also be traced phylogenetically, which means that we can see them across the evolutionary history of the human species. Charles Darwin's work *The Expression of the Emotions in Man and Animals* (1872) is often cited as opening this avenue of investigation. Through analysis of emotional expression in humans and animals, Darwin concludes that much human emotional expression is innate, not learned or socialised (although it can be modified by learning and socialisation), and that different emotional expressions developed at different moments in the evolution of the human, moments connected to various physiological capacities. For instance, because our evolutionary precursors the apes laugh as an expression of pleasure or enjoyment, that emotional expression is quite low on the evolutionary ladder. Higher up – indeed so high as to be uniquely human according to Darwin – are expressions of grief and suffering (in tears); apes do not weep when they suffer.

As interesting as the evolutionary view is, accepting it uncritically would have – and has had – important social consequences that directly affect theatre, its producers, and its audiences. Darwin's first observation, that human emotional expression is innate, minimises the role society and culture play in conditioning feeling and, indeed, in shaping the feeling bodies whose emotional expression is innate. (Let me give a brief, reductive example of how culture might shape feeling bodies: an over-stimulating environment, filled with noise and flashing lights and too many people, amps up the human nervous system, which responds either by over-activating muscles and glands in an effort to keep up with the environmental stimuli or by shutting down in an effort to save itself from burn-out. Over time, this kind of environment can shape bodies that are over/hyper-reactive or 'nervous' because their systems live in a perpetual state of responsiveness.) His second point, that emotional expressions developed at distinct moments in human evolution, ties a hierarchy of emotional expressions to a story of human development. In this scheme, the base emotional expressions most fully articulated through the autonomic nervous system – that is, those that are most bodily and that arose earliest in the evolutionary development of the human species – are associated with animality. They are folded into a repertoire of instinctual reaction that has assured the successful adaptation, and therefore survival, of the species. (If the human species' instinctive response to a bear were aggression instead of flight, there would be no more humans.)

One danger of this evolutionary perspective on feeling is that it grafts a hierarchy of feeling onto a hierarchy of development. Thus, affects such as disgust or sexual excitation are signs of our animal nature, whereas social emotions such as shame or love that involve judgement or discernment are evidence of our more advanced and complete humanity. In short, one becomes more human the higher up the evolutionary/emotional ladder one climbs. These hierarchies also entail a division of body and mind; body occupies the animal end of the spectrum, and mind inhabits the more rarefied and valued human end. As you will see – and as I will try to complicate – this same hierarchy (emotion over affect, human over animal, mind over body) underpins a hierarchy of cultural forms (in which high culture is better than popular culture) to which much affecting theatre falls victim. Furthermore, it sustains a problematic, broader cultural hierarchy that places male above female and white above black on the specious premise that women and people of colour are more 'naturally' 'feeling' creatures (on which more later).

Even in its undeniably bodily qualities and effects, with all its less than flattering bestial connotations, affect also enlightens us as to the import of feeling to theatre. Here's another definition of affect that gestures to that relation, which I'll take up more explicitly later in the section entitled 'Why theatre is': 'affect' refers to an organism's autonomic reaction to an environmental change; this reaction is a subjective experience, meaning that only the person whose blood is rushing to his or her extremities can feel it; this uncontrollable, embodied, individual experience may result in an emotional expression, such as a grimace or wide-eyed paralysis; the emotional expression displays the subjective, affective response in a socially readable way. By casting subjective experience into readable moulds (grimaces, and so on), emotional expression objectifies, if you will, the subjective experience. Thus affect exceeds us thrice over. First, it exceeds us in the sense that it is beyond our control. Second, it is not unique to the individual but is common to the species: increased adrenaline will always sharpen our minds and focus our attention on, for instance, the tightrope walker's hand clinging to a high wire. And third, affect exceeds us in the sense that it may be communicated via emotional display.

Emotion

In the same decade that Duse blushed on the London stage (the 1890s), William James, the father of American psychology and an exponent of what has come to be known as the James—Lange theory of emotion, contended that emotion is the perception of the physiological changes (such as blood rushing to the extremities when a person is angered) of what I've been calling affect. Emotion in this theory is a kind of reflection on or conclusion-drawing from the evidence presented by our bodies and interpreted with the aid of contextual cues. James's most famous illustration of his theory was the imagined situation in which a person is confronted by a bear in the woods. We often think that in response to the bear one first feels afraid and then runs as a consequence of one's fear; James would have it that one sees the bear, runs, and then recognises that the particular way one's body was aroused by and reacted to the bear's presence adds up to 'fear'.

This conclusion-drawing aspect of emotion is precisely where culture – and cultural variation – enters. As an act of interpretation of bodily response, emotion in this formulation is inevitably influenced by a person's expectations and interpretive lens; the shape of the expectations and the curvature of the lens are forged in experience and cultural norms that vary across geography and period. Feminist theatre scholar and playwright Peta Tait's *Performing Emotions: Gender, Bodies, Spaces in Chekhov's Drama and Stanislavski's Theatre* (2002) persuasively advances the claim that emotional expression in theatre is not only hugely culturally variable but also profoundly influenced by gender norms. She defines emotions thus: 'emotions include (emotional) feelings and bodily sensations in the present (momentary) [what I've called "affect" above], which are linked to previously experienced (remembered) voluntary and involuntary patterns of responses and a cognitive system of interpreting these' (p. 16). Thus, until one has either already absorbed a cultural message that bears are dangerous and frightening or had an experience of fear in relation to a bear – and, importantly for us, that experience may be primary (you personally encountered a frightening bear) or vicarious (you witnessed another's frightful encounter with a bear in story, song, or other mode of representation) – one's response to the bear may be one of curiosity or affection or something else entirely. James's bear story is fodder for queer critic Sara Ahmed's reflections on emotion as well. In *The Cultural Politics of Emotion* (2004), she contends that fear is the result neither of something in the person (that is, not the physiological response) nor of something in the bear (a bear is not 'fearsome, "on its own", as it were', Ahmed writes). Rather, fear is 'a matter of how person and bear come into contact' (p. 7). In other words, emotions are relational: fear lies *between* the person and the bear; it is discovered in the person's relation to the bear and the bear's to the person. It is important to keep in mind the relational nature of emotions in our considerations of how theatre produces and, especially, transmits emotion. If emotion is made in the relationship between stage and audience (the stimulus and receiver, if you will), it cannot simply be projected by actors and caught as the same emotion by the audience. The theatre's emotional labour, then, is, in part, a negotiation.

While we must bear in mind emotions' cultural variability, we might also note that the emotions in this view act as a bridge between body and mind, between sensation and evaluation, and indeed between individual and group. In a similar vein to James, though from a more philosophical perspective, Brian Massumi, whose 2002 book *Parables for the Virtual* has become a standard text in critical studies of affect in the humanities, understands emotion as an expression of or name for affective experience; emotion is conventionalised or codified affect, fitted into 'meanings in an intersubjective context' (p. 24). To put our high-wire act experience into an (inevitably reductive) emotion-formula, for instance: (goose pimples + caught breath + widened eyes) × circus = surprise/fear. We take these signs emitted by the autonomic nervous system in the context of a circus performance and interpret them as evidence of the emotions surprise and fear. In this way, as psychologist Keith Oatley puts it in his book *Emotions: A Brief History* (2004), emotions 'occur at the junction of our inner concerns with the outside world' (p. 10). Emotion, then, like affect, moves us out of ourselves by taking subjective experiences and inserting them into a social context of meaning and relation. This is consistent with the earliest recorded usage of the word 'emotion' in English, where it denotes a 'moving out' (from the Latin *emovere*: *e-* 'out' + *movere* 'to move'). Although this usage is now obsolete, the sense of agitation or perturbation indicated by the etymology is still with us where 'emotion' means 'any agitation or disturbance of mind, feeling, passion', as the *Oxford English Dictionary Online* defines it.

Mood

Another class of feeling (mood) prepares us for the specific affective and emotional responses I have detailed above — the gasping, racing hearts and goose pimples associated with a thrill or surprise response and their interpretation as fear. In his useful overview of theories of emotion, *Emotion: The Science of Sentiment* (2001), philosopher Dylan Evans defines moods as 'background states that raise or lower our susceptibility to emotional stimuli' (p. 68). Thus, being in a mood of happy anticipation at attending a circus performance increases your chances of experiencing joy, elation, and thrill in response to the high-wire act. If, on the other hand, you enter the big top in a mood rather darker than the colours of the circus would indicate, you may catch the melancholy of the tramp clown or experience fear and anxiety rather than excitement while watching the high-wire act. Cultivating a receptive mood in audiences that may enhance their experience of a given act has often been a job for theatrical music – produced by the circus band or, in many nineteenth-century popular entertainments such as melodrama, music hall, and vaudeville, by the pit orchestra. Composer Miriam Cutler attributes the success of her music for Circus Flora, a small new American circus based in St Louis, Missouri, to its ability to create a common mood. In an interview with circus historian Ernest Albrecht in *The Contemporary Circus* (2006), she says, 'To me, there's no finer moment than when the audience is clapping with the music in time with an act. That, to me, means I'm doing my job, and the band is doing their job. The act is happy and the audience is happy; everyone is in one space' (p. 84). At the opposite end of the mood spectrum, think of how the soundtrack to a horror film can create a sense of foreboding that heightens the spectator's affective response to the serial killer's sudden emergence from the closet (or what have you). Turn the sound down, and the action appears almost comical in its jerky camera movements and sudden physical actions.

A quick summary, now, of the categories of feeling that endow theatre with its vitality and its vital necessity to those who love it. Affect happens *to* us (remember, it is out of our conscious control) and yet happens *through* us (it is the body regulating itself via the activation of certain organs, processes, or responses, as when we shiver in the cold). Mood is a disposition or background state that orients us to certain kinds of emotional responses and reactions. And emotion names our sensate, bodily experience in a way that at once organises it and makes it legible to ourselves and consonant with others' experiences or emotional lives. Each of these categories of feeling is a response to stimuli of some kind, and each helps us navigate our world in its base realities, such as bears in the woods or a chill in the air, and in its complex social situations, such as family reunions or higher education. Each also moves us out of ourselves: affect by its occurrence against our will, mood by its ambient nature, and emotion by its communicative and relational properties. These two principles – that feelings are stimulus responses and that they extend our perception beyond our own body and its situation – form the basis for feeling's centrality to theatre, the subject of the next section.

Why theatre is: connections to the body and brain

Sense perception

We've seen that feelings are bodily responses to the stimulus of changes in our environment, both external (as in the bear) and internal (as in our mood). For its part, the theatre offers 'super-stimuli'; that is, it concentrates and amplifies the world's natural sensory effects. As such, feeling is particularly provoked by theatre. This, then, might be the first way in which theatre and feeling are fundamentally tied: the extra-stimulating stimuli of the theatre directly address feelings (emotions, moods, affect, sensations) and, in so doing, draw out extraordinary affective response. I've

noted already the expanded emotional repertoire used in
and activated by the bigger-than-life aspects of the theatre
as plots move characters from emotional peaks to emotional valleys, from the pride of kingship to the shame of
exile. So let us regard here for a moment the super-stimuli
of the visual aspects of theatrical performance as well. For
example, red has the physiological effect of revving us up;
as the traditional red dining room might indicate, red can
increase heart rate and trigger a hunger response. In the
natural world, red generally punctuates our visual field –
poppies dotting the countryside, berries on a bush, a fiery
yet ephemeral sunset; in the theatre, however, designers
might flood the spectator's visual field with red, thereby
turning a natural stimulus into a super-stimulus and, consequently, heightening the spectator's feeling. *The Poor of
New York* (Wallack's Theater, New York, 1857) by Irish
playwright and producer Dion Boucicault included a red
wall of fire, connecting the principle of colour's super-
stimulus properties to the response of surprise and fear at
fire in an enclosed, crowded public space. In an article in
Scientific American ('Illusions of the Stage', 1881), Boucicault
describes how he achieved the illusion of the Act 5 con-
flagration of a tenement building (notably, like the theatre, an enclosed, crowded space). A combination of 'flash
torches' of a quick-burning powder called lycopodium and
'a very large endless towel upon which is printed a mass
of flames ... [which is] kept in constant motion' behind the
tenement frontage and glimpsed through its windows created the sensational effect (pp. 4265–66). To this he added

a large cast of supernumeraries in firemen's uniforms; not coincidentally, these uniforms, which are depicted in a set of lithographs from 1854, feature red shirts. The early twentieth-century Russian Expressionist painter Wassily Kandinsky also exploited this principle of super-stimulus in his 'colour-tone dramas', written between 1909 and 1914 (though not staged as planned at the time, owing to the outbreak of World War I). In *The Yellow Sound*, published in *The Blaue Reiter Almanac* [The Blue Rider Almanac], edited by Kandinsky and fellow painter Franz Marc ([1912] 1974), among the characters, who are costumed in single colours, are five 'intensely yellow giants (as large as possible)'. After their '*very* deep singing without words' in Picture 1 (of the 6 'pictures' that make up the play), the 'front of the stage becomes blue and more and more opaque ... [then] a thick blue fog completely obscures the stage' (p. 213). In these two cases, Kandinsky and Boucicault expanded colour from a point of punctuation to fill the visual field and, thereby, increased its affective impact.

Yet the fundamental centrality of feeling to theatre is not seen only in the theatre's production of super-stimuli to strong effect. The whole enterprise of theatre is geared to the perceiving body; it is directional communication generally between actors and spectators that *exists to be perceived*. Stanton Garner is a theatre phenomenologist – that is, someone who adopts the philosophical practice of studying phenomena (things) as they appear to, and are experienced by, individuals. In *Bodied Spaces* (1994), he argues, 'It is through the actor's corporeal presence under the spectator's gaze that the dramatic text actualizes itself in the field of performance' (p. 1). Avant-garde director Peter Brook similarly isolates the most basic components of theatre in *The Empty Space* (1968): 'A man walks across this empty space whilst someone else is watching him, and this is all that is needed for an act of theatre to be engaged' (p. 9). In other words, at its most fundamental, the act of theatre requires two sentient bodies: one to act, another to apprehend. Although theatre exists to be perceived – as it exists only in being perceived – it also presents an important challenge to perception. Indeed, feminist performance theorist Peggy Phelan defines the ontology (that is, being or essence) of performance as *dis*appearance. (While this may seem contrary to Garner's and Brook's positions, she still approaches the definition of theatrical performance in the terms of perception.) She argues in her book *Unmarked: The Politics of Performance* (1993) that because each live performance is unique ('performance occurs over a time that will not be repeated', she says on page 146), live performance is defined by its 'plunge into visibility' and its subsequent disappearance. Put differently, live performance toys with our perceptual abilities: it is there before our eyes and ears and then, almost instantly, it is gone. It is that quality of being here and then gone, available to and then removed from perception, that constitutes performance.

It is important to remember, however, that even though in most conventional theatre set-ups one body acts while another body watches, both those bodies – actor and spectator – are simultaneously objects of perception and perceiving beings. To this point, Garner observes that theatre is a 'bodied space' in two fundamental ways: first, it is populated by bodies (actors, spectators); second, those bodies are not just there to be perceived – as when spectators gaze upon actors – but also have the capacity for perception themselves. (Again, perception refers to the faculty of apprehending by means of the senses, or awareness of environmental elements via sensation.) First, actors are objects of the perception of the audience, who listen to the lines the actors recite and watch their onstage adventures. Second, actors are also responding to the cues offered by their onstage and back-stage peers, as well as to those emitted by the audience in the form of, say, uncomfortable pauses where laughs should be or the rustle of cough drops being liberated from their paper chrysalises. Trained to be hyper-responsive to environmental changes around them (on which more later), actors have finely tuned perceptive faculties.

To the audience, whose perceptive abilities are generally less acute, the modern material practices of theatre production offer assistance by guiding spectator perception towards that to which they might profitably and enjoyably pay attention. The theatre does this by, for instance, illuminating the stage more brightly than the house, removing the audience from the stage area (both relatively recent practices inaugurated in England by the eminent actor, playwright, and theatre manager David Garrick at his Drury Lane theatre in the mid-eighteenth century), and, more recently, requesting that patrons turn off their mobile phones during the show. In these ways, the technologies of the theatre are used as what I'll call 'feeling-technologies', or mechanisms that do something with feeling. In these examples, the feeling-technologies of lighting, architecture, and audience control orient the spectator's senses – notably, her vision and hearing – to the action onstage by effectively reducing the number of stimuli competing with the onstage performance. Even in the English Restoration theatre, which did have select members of the audience seated onstage and uniform (candle) light across the stage and the house, the audience's attention was directed to the speaking actor by her taking up a position downstage centre. That that particular actor was *acting* – and thus might be worthy of audience attention – was marked as well by the actors who surrounded her; those other actors would have been very occupied with *not* acting. Most Restoration actors dropped character when not called upon to speak their lines; while their colleagues acted around them, they would chat up attractive people in the side boxes close to the stage or appear bored, distracted, or generally disengaged from the play going on around them until they heard their cue to act. The powerful downstage centre position, if no longer the only stage location at which acting takes place, is still frequently used to indicate a character's significance and interest. Curtain calls are often staged such that actors emerge from an upstage line or from the wings to occupy that position, from which they bow; contemporary musical theatre soloists often command centre stage – and generally a spotlight picks them out of a darkened or at least muted visual surround – for their big numbers.

The bodied space of theatre, then, organises itself around our sentient beings on both sides of the proverbial footlights, by highlighting the stage's stimulating properties and by directing the audience's perceptual faculties towards them. This constitutes a crucial part of theatre's feeling-labour: by offering super-stimuli, theatre solicits or activates feeling responses in the audience; by focusing the audience's attention, theatre manages the nature and moment of the audience's feeling response, potentially orchestrating it into a common, collective response, such as I experienced when the high-wire performer missed his landing. (As it turns out, his was an intentional though convincing bungle.) This is part of the design of theatre. And clearly there is a logic to the fact that if we made it, it should serve, affect, or please us. But as both new scientific breakthroughs and old phenomenology demonstrate, theatrical imitation puts our sensuous faculties – feeling – at its centre because it emanates from them and, in a spookily real way, is part of them. As we've seen in this section, theatre *stimulates* our feeling responses. In the next section, I'll show how theatre also *simulates* (or mimics) the neurological basis of our feeling responses. Let me explain.

The theatrical brain

In 1996, a group of Italian neuroscientists at the University of Parma discovered a set of neurons in the premotor cortex of the brains of macaques that became active 'both when the monkey performed a given action and when it observed a similar action performed by the experimenter' (Vittorio Gallese et al., 'Action Recognition in the Premotor Cortex', p. 593). (Neuroimaging studies in humans show these neurons to be present in our brains as well.) In other words, the observation of another's action – say, grasping a high wire – activates the same neurons that would light up if the observer grasped a high wire herself; her observation of another person's grasping generates a 'motor representation' of grasping in her brain. In other words, this class of neurons reproduce the neural component of the observed movement; they create a representation in the brain of the observed action (in the form of a set of activated neurons). We might say they produce a literal mental image of the observed action. Neuroscientists call these 'mirror neurons' to signify their role in mirroring or imitating the neural make-up of the action they observe. Subsequent experiments have revealed that what is true for motor representation of action in the brain is also true for neural representation of emotion in the brain. In a 2003 article published in *Neuron*, the University of Parma researchers, in conjunction with a team of French neuroscientists, posited a theory of emotional replication (Bruno Wicker et al., 'Both of Us Disgusted in My Insula'). Study participants first inhaled odours producing the affect of disgust; they then viewed film of people expressing disgust via their facial expressions. In both instances, the same neural clusters fired in their brain. When they observed expressions of disgust, participants' mirror neurons created a neural *representation* (or mental image) of disgust indistinguishable from the actual *experience* of disgust at a putrid smell. To the human brain, observation and experience – or, put differently, simulation and reality – are, effectively, the same thing.

Of the several conclusions scientists have drawn from the ongoing research into mirror neurons, one especially relevant to theatre studies is the claim made by Vittorio Gallese, Christian Keysers, and Giacomo Rizzolatti in 'A Unifying View of the Basis of Social Cognition' (2004): the mirror neurons' 'direct simulation of the observed events' grants people 'a direct experiential grasp of the mind of others' (p. 396). Thus, some neuroscientists believe we can apprehend, and indeed experience vicariously, what another person is doing or feeling courtesy of mirror neurons. We live through another's experience via the mental images of that experience produced in areas of the cortex involved in motor control. The brain, then, operates like a small theatre, producing representations of action and emotion that are not necessarily *executed* by their audience but are nonetheless electrically *experienced* by them.

In its production of affecting representations, the brain mimics the operations of a theatre. The theatre, in turn, imitates that fundamental brain function. In its simulation of brain function, theatre performs another kind of feeling-labour – namely, meeting a basic need for connection. To explain, we'll follow the work of theatre phenomenologist Bert O. States in *The Pleasure of the Play* (1994). States found in concerted neuronal firings (such as those of the mirror neurons) a primary impetus for theatrical representation in

31

the brain's production of 'mental objects' or images. Citing the research of brain biologist Jean-Pierre Changeux, States notes that a basic activity of the human brain – and one that it spends a good deal of time engaging in, apparently – is the making of representations or 'mental pictures'. States speculates that these mental pictures form the 'biological precedent' to art, and specifically to theatre. The theory goes that in order to compensate for the profound interiority of these mental pictures – their inscription on the cortex, as it were – we seek to give them external representation in the form of art. In States's words, 'we are driven to produce equivalences ... which are, in a certain sense, imitations of neuronal feelings' (p. 20). In this way, our fleeting, internal mental images become more durable, external objects for our observation, contemplation, and manipulation. Here, then, art – or, more to our point, theatre – performs the emotional labour of giving form and expression to human mental experience. This exteriorisation or objectivisation (the rendering of something abstract such as a mental image as a concrete object) of neuronal images not only satisfies our need to give evidence to our individual emotional lives but also performs a more fundamental emotional service: it satisfies the basic human emotional need for connection, for feeling not-alone. In this context, art is a mechanism by which we might overcome what States terms 'our ontological isolation from the things of the world' (p. 22).

To begin to unpack this elemental feeling-labour afforded by the art of the theatre, consider first the question: How do the senses contribute to one's feeling of isolation from (and in) the world?

It is our senses — touch, taste, smell, sight, hearing — that tell us we are distinct from the world; they define and patrol our physical perimeter by registering the effects of the world on our selves. (As I've said several times here already, they flare when there is a change in their environment.) We live, then, with near-constant reminders that we are separate from our surroundings; they may encompass us, but they are not *of* us. Interestingly, that which patrols our isolation — namely the affect system, which comprises the physiological and cognitive dimensions discussed in this section — also breaks it open. Imitations (in the brain and in the worldly form of art) can help fill that gap between the self and the world because they hover, perceptually, between the self and the world; they participate in and are the consequence of both. How so? Because theatre is an imitation that uses the materials of the life-world to create its symbolic world. Take Willy Loman. In Miller's character we have a picture or imitation of a middle-aged, middle-American salesman of the mid-twentieth century. You can see already in my description of him how 'Willy' imitates or mirrors real kinds of people, those actual middle-aged, middle-American salesmen of the mid-twentieth century. So Willy-the-character is crafted, in part, out of real-world elements.

More concrete might be the example of his costuming in the original production: a slightly rumpled, dark three-piece suit, worn with a white shirt, patterned tie, and black dress shoes. There was a pen in the right waistcoat pocket. The pen, suit, shirt, tie, shoes, and so on that make up the costume of Willy Loman are also just a pen, suit, shirt, tie, shoes, and so on. The pen is Willy's pen – handy in the event of a sale being made, an order placed – but it is also a pen such as any of us might use to take notes. Theatre – and perhaps this is its magic – drafts this ordinary pen from our world into the fiction of *Death of a Salesman*, where it is never used and where its never being used accrues tragic significance for Willy. In its conscription to the world of Miller's salesman (and the play is framed as Willy's dream world, remember – its original title was *Inside of His Head*), the pen exists somewhere between the world from which it is drawn and the self of the creator or spectator who endows it with meaning. In States's words, these imitations of theatre 'are collusions between objective nature and subjective holdings of the private brain: they are both fictitious and real' (p. 19). The pen is both fictitious (it is a fictional character's fictional pen, if you will) and real (it's still a pen).

In the theatre's material aspects, then, in its redeployment of things such as pens, theatre's imitations are of this world. But they are also of other worlds – the imaginative worlds of the stage that have their own boundaries, logics, and types. Moreover, as evidence from the mirror neuron experiments suggests, theatre's imitations arouse other worlds again (in the form of mental pictures) in the spectator's brain. The pleasure of viewing such theatrical imitations, States continues, 'arises from a dimension of actuality in which the self and the other are joined and exchange natures, thus offering a momentary solution to the enigma of our ontological isolation from the things of the world' (pp. 19–20). Of this phenomenon, French sociologist Émile Durkheim writes in 'The Dualism of Human Nature and Its Social Conditions' (1964), 'It is only by expressing their feelings, by translating them into signs, by symbolizing them externally, that the individual consciousnesses, which are, by nature, closed to each other, can feel that they are communicating and in unison' (p. 336). So, imitations make us feel connected to our environment in a way that is not merely stimulus–response, which, at the same time, reinforces our severance from the world around us (because we are responding to something not of us). Furthermore, imitations make us feel connected to other selves in our world by virtue of our brain's replication of the neuronal basis (or biological precedent) of what we observe on others' faces; the neuronal pathways that trigger certain facial expressions light up in the viewer's mind, too, upon seeing those facial expressions. We might think of artistic production as the senses' way of compensating for the feeling of aloneness produced by their daily stimulation.

So theatre stimulates our affect system, copies our brain function, and, in so doing, allows us to move out of our ontological isolation, to connect with what and who is around us. In these ways, theatre is bound up with feeling in the most elemental way. In addition, it meets one of our most basic needs – that of connection or belonging. Bear in mind that feeling connected to other people is not only a basic psychological need (there's a sound if obviously twisted logic to using isolation as a torture practice); it also ensures that other basic needs (food, water, sleep) are met. How? Because it cements care-giving and interdependent relationships, which are especially crucial in the vulnerable first years of life. In sum, then, in its super-stimuli, theatre appeals to our sense perception; in its mechanics, it guides the same. And at the level of brain biology, theatre builds upon and then feeds back to the images of mirror neurons, neurons that allow us to experience vicariously another's internal life, which is the basis of theatrical satisfaction.

Feeling as the purpose of theatre

The feeling body is theatre's focus: theatre requires a perceiving person in order to *be*. The feeling body is also the vehicle for theatre's images and execution. The feeling body is, then, both the basis and the means of theatre. This may be a unifying condition or definition of theatre. However, the feeling body has as often acted as a dividing line. What role does feeling play with respect to the purpose of theatre? How might theatre best manage the vicarious experience it generates? To what ends should this sensate body at the core of theatrical representation and reception be put? I find the cognitive neuroscience stuff with which we ended the previous section fascinating for what it suggests about how we process, respond to, and generate the theatre's sensory enchantments, and for what it suggests about the ways in which theatre's feeling-labour meets certain basic needs (such as human connection). But it is not the last word on theatre and feeling, even if it is the latest approach to take the study of emotion and its expression by storm. And again, like evolutionary science-based theories of emotion and emotional expression, this work has been criticised for sidelining the impact of culture and context on brain biology. Numerous scientists remind us that the *nature* of the brain is decidedly influenced by the *nurture* of its environment. Neurobiologist Lise Eliot, in *Pink Brain, Blue Brain* (2009), warns against an overly deterministic view of the brain as unalterable 'nature'. Her review of the science of sex difference and brain biology – science that indicates that there are no significant biological sex differences in the brain (thus, boys are not wired to be better at math, and girls are not 'naturally' more empathetic) – reminds us just how mouldable the brain is. Brains change and develop in relation to their surroundings, physical and social. Over time, then, gender differences that are reinforced in the family, at school, and in the culture at large help to create 'pink' and 'blue' brains. In 'Against Simulation' (2005), Harvard University psychologist Rebecca Saxe takes aim specifically at the 'simulation theory' of the mind, which holds that mirror neurons allow for 'understanding the meaning of the actions and emotions of others by internally replicating ("simulating") them without any explicit mediation' (Gallese et al., 'A Unifying View', p. 396). Despite acknowledging the theory's 'powerful insights into the neural representation of simple actions and some basic emotions (most plausibly, disgust and fear)', Saxe maintains that because of environmental differences between actor and observer, the observer's brain is an unreliable template for the actor's. She writes, 'An observer never has exactly the same perspective, or information, as the actor does. Could differences in the inputs (such as what features of the context are represented and how) lead to differences between the real, and the simulated, outputs of decision-making and reasoning?' (p. 178). In short, even if we all begin with the same wiring, if you will, our own brain's particular, context-influenced wiring is not necessarily predictive of another's.

In this section, then, I'll buttress my claim that feeling furnishes the theatre with its *raison d'être* from another angle – from within theatre studies – by examining what dramatic and performance theory has had to say about theatre's purpose, particularly in relation to feeling. (Just briefly, dramatic theory is thinking which undertakes a systematic generalising from theatrical practice to produce statements of general principles regarding the aims, methods, functions, and characteristics of theatre. Dramatic theory often searches for rules or norms that govern 'good' dramatic practice.) For although I think it hard to deny that doing things with feeling is, at the very least, an important function of theatre – whether or not that functionality is proven via brain biology – it is something else again to assert that doing things with feeling is what theatre is *for*. In fact, my claim that theatre exists to perform crucial and necessary feeling-labour amounts to picking a side in a debate over the purpose of theatre that is more than two millennia old.

In a versified letter called *Ars Poetica* (The Art of Poetry) dating from the first century BCE and addressed to two young would-be playwrights, the Roman author Horace set out to define and prescribe the elements of a good play. These include character consistency, likeness to real-world models (thus, old men should be depicted as cranky, for instance!), a five-act structure, and the relegation of the obscene or incredible to the *ob-skene* (offstage) so as not to offend or strain the audience's belief in the dramatic fiction. However, his most influential comment concerns the very purpose of drama: 'The poet's aim is either to profit or to please.' In this context, 'profit' denotes a 'benefit', as it is sometimes translated. As such, a playwright's goal is either to benefit the audience, usually by offering a lesson or instructive example, or to amuse them, generally through sensory and emotional satisfactions.

You can see already how Horace separates theatre's two purposes on what I've been arguing is theatre's ground: feeling. Profit tends to be allied with the mind and with rational activity; pleasure usually takes up with the body and, in so doing, engages more directly with feeling in all its valences. It would be a mistake, however, to assume that theatre of profit is devoid of feeling. The difference between the two kinds of theatre – profitable and pleasurable – is one of degree, not one of kind. Both perform feeling-labour. But they do so to different extents, with different purposes, and with different outcomes. Let's begin our discussion of feeling in relation to theatre's dual (and often duelling) purposes as sketched by Horace with a look into how an exemplary theatre of profit – ancient Greek tragedy – makes, manages, and distributes feelings by forging a subdued and rationalised relation to the feeling body.

Profit

Notice, first, how the formal organisation of the tragedies – the way the plays were put together – acts as a feeling-technology (again, a theatrical mechanism that does something with feeling – directs sense perception, increases or dampens emotional response in the audience, creates a mood, and so on). A key feature of Greek tragedies, and one not often used in modern theatrical practice, is the Chorus, thought to have been made up of twelve to fifteen performers, who chanted and moved in choreographed unison at intervals throughout the plays. Their poetic passages structurally separate dramatic incidents (or events) with rumination on those incidents. Thus, the more spectacular and affecting present-tense dramatic action, which is performed by the named actors (Antigone, Medea, Oedipus), alternates with the reflective passages of the Chorus.

The feeling-technology of alternating episodes not only separates incident from reflection in Greek tragedy; it also mitigates or otherwise digests the incidents and their affecting effects. For example, in the final scene of Sophocles' *Oedipus Rex* (Theatre Dionysus, Athens, 431 BCE), Oedipus, the king of Thebes, emerges from the palace; his eyes have been gouged out by his own hand, and his face is consequently bloodied. This visually striking and emotionally shocking moment is prepared for by the Messenger, who recounts the terrible offstage events of the self-blinding just before Oedipus' appearance. When

Oedipus emerges, the Chorus responds to and interprets the awful scene: 'This is a terrible sight for men to see! / I never found a worse! / ... Indeed I pity you, but I cannot / look at you, though there's much I want to ask / and much to learn and much to see' (ll. 1298–1306). The spectators live the blinding three times, as it were: first, through the messenger's description of Oedipus' action; second, by seeing the painful consequences of those events in the bloodied mask of Oedipus; and, third, by hearing the Chorus's response to them. Notably, the presumably sensational scene of Oedipus blinding himself with Jocasta's broaches is kept offstage, out of the view of the *theatron* ('seeing place'). The play closes with the Chorus's summary of the lesson – or profit – to be taken away from the performance: 'You that live in my ancestral Thebes, behold this Oedipus, – / him who knew the famous riddles and was a man most masterful; / not a citizen who did not look with envy on his lot – / see him now and see the breakers of misfortune swallow him! / Look upon that last day always. Count no mortal happy till / he has passed the final limit of his life secure from pain' (ll. 1524–30).

This is not to reduce *Oedipus Rex* to a parable. Rather, it is to spotlight how Greek tragedy manages its sensory appeals – particularly its appeals to ungovernable affects such as surprise or disgust – by channelling them through (or substituting them for) reflection or cogitation in tragedy's form and content. Even the actions seen onstage are, effectively, acts of cognition or of language: Oedipus makes a decision; Creon reasons with Oedipus; Tiresias pronounces the oracle; Jocasta implores her husband to leave well enough alone; and so on. Moreover, Oedipus' acts of cognition and of language (his speech-act of promising Thebes he'll find and punish Laius's murderer, for instance) are resolutely *not* attentive to the body; indeed, his promise and subsequent investigation ignore the case's most glaring evidence: his own swollen foot (the literal meaning of his very name, 'Oedipus'), which indicates that he is the baby whose ankles Jocasta and Laius had pinned and who was sent to Cithaeron to die. There is a certain irony to the fact that a resolutely bodied art form such as theatre – a place of sense perception – has at the foundation of its Western canon a play that eschews bodily knowledge in its construction as well as in its main, exemplary character. Indeed, the irony is even richer when one considers that Oedipus not only overlooks bodily knowledge but also punishes himself by eliminating one of his senses. Instead, *Oedipus Rex* emphasises abstracted thinking over the evidence of the physical body; its feeling-technologies operate in a way that sublimates feeling.

Pleasure

At the other end of the profit–pleasure (and, implicitly, cognition–feeling) spectrum sit those forms that solicit most actively, obviously, or consistently an audience's feelings – whether they are affects such as thrills and chills, moods such as melancholy and happiness, or emotions such as joy and despair. For our example of a 'pleasing' theatrical form, let us take nineteenth-century melodrama, unarguably the dominant theatrical form of that century across Europe and the Americas. (And for melodrama sceptics, I'll just note that 'pleasing' here is used in its expansive sense of 'activating affects and/or emotions'. In other words, you don't have to like melodrama to read this next bit.) Melodrama is a theatrical form that evidently aims to please. As literary critic Peter Brooks puts it in *The Melodramatic Imagination* (1976), melodrama is unsubtle in its address to the senses and emotions; it 'handles its feelings and ideas virtually as plastic entities'. Emotions in melodrama are 'visual and tactile models held out for all to see and to handle' (p. 41). You might know melodramatic conventions best through their latter-day kin, television soap operas. The typical melodramatic plot line is based in the conflict between good and evil or virtue and vice; virtuous good triumphs, of course, as evidence of a providential ethos. Melodrama has the benefit (some would say handicap) of abundantly clear characterisation; heroes and villains are studies in contrast – the former completely good and the latter absolutely bad. Character contrasts were immediately legible in their typical costuming (this is the form that gave us the black-hatted villain and the white-dressed heroine, for instance) and in the musical motifs that accompanied their entrances. In the absence of nuanced psychology, melodrama's characters wear their thoughts and emotions all over their bodies in the form of significant postures, gestures, and vocal intonations.

The features sketched above make melodrama as a form somewhat laughable today for its narrative implausibility (how many babies could reasonably have been switched at birth, for instance, and how many people of unimpeachable moral character could have been easily identified by a tell-tale scar or birthmark?), the predictability of its plot formulae, and the breathless expressions of its characters ('Oh, the pangs, the dreadful pangs that tear the sailor's wife, as, wakeful on her tear-wet pillow, she lists and trembles at the roaring sea!'). As hackneyed as they may seem today, however, melodramas such as Douglas Jerrold's *Black Ey'd Susan*, whose eponymous heroine I've quoted just above (p. 109), were smash hits. (As another indication of melodrama's embrace of sensory perception, note that this play's title character, Susan, is identified by her black eyes; whereas Oedipus destroys his perceptual apparatus, Susan's appears constitutive of her identity.) This particular 'Nautical and Domestic Drama in Two Acts' opened in June 1829 at the Royal Surrey Theatre, London, where it ran for more than four hundred nights at a time when an average run was one week (Louis James, 'Taking Melodrama Seriously', 1977, p. 152). It made the careers of the playwright and his leading man; T. P. Cooke, who played Black Ey'd Susan's true love, the British sailor William, performed this, his most popular role until he was seventy-four years old! What could be the attraction? I would argue that melodrama cultivates a close, provocative relationship to feeling in a formal apparatus that invokes physical responses in predictable, formulaic, familiar – and therefore reassuring – patterns. Indeed, melodrama may be usefully understood as a kind of feeling-producing machine, formally engineered to elicit emotional response. In other words, melodrama appeals because it has mastered the theatrical craft of pleasing and, as such, achieves its purpose – sometimes with a vengeance.

We saw in the example from Boucicault's *The Poor of New York* how scenography and scenic effects such as the tenement fire can be used as a feeling-technology which, via its super-stimuli, arouses the intense affective response of the autonomous nervous system. In contrast to Greek tragedy, here the feeling-technology is used not to douse the flames of feeling but to fan them in order to produce a sense of wonder. Melodrama of the nineteenth-century English stage possessed an entire arsenal of feeling-technologies intended to whip up enthusiasm.

To begin to understand the workings of melodrama's feeling-technologies, let's take the example of plot. In *Black Ey'd Susan*, the plot amounts to a series of assaults (or attempted assaults) on Susan's honour and on the life of William, her loving husband. In the first scene, Susan's Uncle Doggrass imperils her by threatening to turn her out into the winter cold if she does not come up with the rent immediately. Doggrass has already ensured that his orphan niece (it's not enough that he persecutes her despite their blood relationship; her parents have to have died as well to amp up the pathos) will be unable to pay the rent by having her only protector, William, shipped off with the navy. Doggrass's financial offensive is then matched by two sexual offensives – the first by a smuggler and trading partner of Doggrass named Hatchet and the second by William's commanding officer, Captain Crosstree, drunk on wine and 'passion' at the time of his aggressive overture. Then it's William's turn to have his virtue besmirched. In saving Susan from the Captain's unwanted advances, William, ignorant of the Captain's identity, strikes him with a cutlass and gravely injures him. So follows a trial for attempted murder of a superior officer at which William is pronounced guilty and sentenced to death by hanging. Only the last-minute appearance of the wounded Crosstree saves William's life: 'I alone am the culprit – 'twas I who would have dishonoured him. [...] He saved my life; I had written for his discharge – villainy has kept back the document. [...] When William struck me he was not the King's sailor – I was not his officer' (p. 137). The villain who kept back the exonerating letter was, of course, Doggrass. With this vindication, William is released, his truly virtuous character fully revealed by the logic of the plot. He is joined in the stage-picture by his wife, equally resplendent in her saved virtue, while the seamen cheer and music sounds. In other words, and as Brooks has argued, the melodramatic form ensures virtue and goodness emerge from the obfuscating mists of threat and false accusation to appear, shiny and in public, as recognisably themselves. For this reason, Brooks contends, melodramatic 'conflict and structure do not exist merely for pathos and thrills, and the peripeties [reversals of situation] and *coups de théâtre* [spectacular effects] are not extrinsic to the moral issues as melodrama conceives them. On the contrary, ... melodrama typically not only employs virtue persecuted as a source of its dramaturgy, but also tends to become the dramaturgy of virtue misprized and eventually recognised' (*The Melodramatic Imagination*, pp. 26–27).

Now couple the Manichaean character portraits (William's and Susan's pure virtue; Doggrass's evident evil) and the polarised conflict between good and evil of the dramatic situation — both of which enable heightened dramatic conflict and emotional expression, itself codified in a exaggerated repertoire of physical gesture — with an emotionally explosive, even hyperbolic, use of language, another technology of feeling. Listen to William when he thinks Susan is not at the port to meet him upon his return from sea: 'I'm afraid to throw out a signal — my heart knocks against my timbers, like a jolly-boat in a breeze, alongside a seventy-four. Damn it, I feel as if one half of me were in the Baltic, and the other half stationed in Jamaica' (p. 117). Not only is the audience made to understand the details of William's confused emotional life in this moment, but that life is articulated in an overstated version of sea-faring language. Of William's idiom, theatre historian Maurice Willson Disher writes in *Blood and Thunder* (1949) that 'no other seaman [was] so redolent of tar, so virtuous compared with landsmen, so full of sea-faring oaths, exclamations, similes and metaphors — salt water is rarely out of their [melodrama's seamen's] mouths and often fills their eyes' (pp. 143–44). Indeed, William's tears are another sign of his virtue. The fact that he is a man of feeling betokens his naturalness and full humanity. Contrast this with Doggrass's approach to feeling. The comic woman, Dolly Mayflower, calls Doggrass to account for his cold-hearted treatment of his niece, asking, 'So, Mr. Doggrass, this is how you behave to unfortunate folks — coming and selling them up, and turning them out. Is this your feeling for the poor?' Doggrass retorts, 'Feeling! I pay the rates' (p. 111). A hardnosed businessman (and crook), Doggrass signals his villainy to the audience through his unrepentant lack of feeling.

Here, feeling is aligned specifically with a moral precept of sympathy for the less fortunate. But more generally, and understood to include an expansive range of emotional and affective responses, feeling is the real hero of much nineteenth-century melodrama. To feel – that is, to be physiologically responsive to your environment (affect), to experience ambient mood, and to interpret your body's physiological signals as emotions – is to be human in the most flattering sense of the term. Melodrama's governing Christian ethos would remind viewers that to be human is to be made in the image of God. Feeling along with the characters, being moved by the stirring and patriotic naval tunes, sympathising with Susan's predicament, rooting for her besting of Doggrass, and rejoicing in her permanent reunion with her husband, William, proved the audience's capacity for human feeling as well.

It would be well to recall the evolutionary theory of emotion and its pitfalls here, for we see its operation in melodrama's placing of the capacity for emotion (especially social emotions such as pity for those less fortunate and love of family) at the apex of human development. Remember: William cries; apes don't. If this works in William's favour – he displays his full, feeling humanity every time salt water comes up into his eyes – it does not operate the same way for other character types. For some, feeling places them at the bottom of that evolutionary ladder. There is an odd interlude in the last scene of Act 1 of *Black Ey'd Susan* that merits our attention in this regard. William and Susan are at a public house with friends and neighbours when William is asked about the provenance of his tobacco box. In response, William tells a story about St Domingo Billy, a shark that swam around his fleet of boats anchored off Santa Domingo, Dominican Republic, in the West Indies. In the story, the 'little black baby' of a 'black bumboat woman' – that is, a West Indian woman carrying provisions from the port to the naval vessels in her small craft – 'jumped out of its mother's grappling and landed in Billy's jaws' (p. 125). William's comrade rescues the baby by jumping into the water, cutting open the shark, and retrieving the baby from its guts.

What possible dramatic purpose could the telling of this tale serve? As a colourful tale of life at sea, it fits into the entertaining environment of the public house, to be sure, where the revellers drink, sing (the popular song about black-ey'd Susan that prompted the melodrama), and dance, in addition to listening to William's adventure. But it does nothing whatsoever to advance the plot or to delineate character; after all, the story is not about William's heroism but about his peer Tom's. Moreover, the bumboat woman and her child seem almost incidental to the tale. The mother's and baby's perspectives of the situation are not filled in, and their story of separation and reunion is left unfinished. The last image of the baby's mother that William offers his listeners is of her giving 'a shriek that would have split the boatswain's whistle!' as the baby falls into the shark's mouth. The last image of the baby is of it being held by a triumphant Tom, who has '[come] up, all over blood with the little baby in his hand, and the shark turned over dead upon its side' (p. 125). And once Tom has surfaced, all attention turns to the shark, whose gut yields things of greater interest to the sailors, and presumably to William's listeners, than the endangered baby: watches, tobacco boxes, an Admiral's hat, and pilots' telescopes.

Here is one moment where attention to feeling, its circulation, and its associations is rewarded; for that which cannot be sufficiently explained through its meaning might be illuminated through its feeling-labour. I've pointed already to the entertainment value of the tale; it features many of the pleasing aspects of melodrama: an innocent victim, a heroic action, a family reunited. But the story of the baby is also just a pretext for the exciting revelation of other emotional values. First, it highlights again the British navy sailor's feeling for humanity (his evolved social emotions), and thus his fully actualised humanity; it is notably not the mother who goes in after her baby but Tom who is moved to help. This contrasts the presumably white male sailor ('presumably white' because his race is left unremarked) with the black bumboat woman, who does not have a name in the story other than her racial descriptor and occupation and whose response to the alarming situation is reduced to a panic response (an affective response), signalled in an almost inhuman shriek. We see, then, the evolutionary hierarchy of Darwinian emotion theory at work, in which the black woman is linked to the more resolutely physical experiences of affect (again, she is not depicted feeling relief or gratitude or love at the return of her infant) and the white man demonstrates a broader and more advanced emotional repertoire (see also José Esteban Muñoz, 'Feeling Brown', 2001, and Ahmed, *The Cultural Politics of Emotion*, on how affect gets ascribed to people of colour).

Second, just as the baby's jeopardy affords sailor Tom the chance to display his heroism – Tom is 'as fine a seaman as ever stept', in William's account (p. 125) – putting the story in William's mouth helps create the impression of British navy sailors as *typically* heroic saviours of the imperilled. The sailor as hero, liberator, and 'good guy' was a common enough trope in the nautical melodramas so popular at the Surrey Theatre where *Black Ey'd Susan* played. Hazel Waters writes, 'The sailor was *the* working-class dramatic hero, defender of England and of the oppressed' (p. 52, emphasis in original). But, as her book *Racism on the Victorian Stage* (2007) attests, English liberty – along with its sailor liberators – was often thrown into dramatic relief through its contrast with the enslavement of black peoples. Although the bumboat woman in *Black Ey'd Susan* is depicted not as a slave but as a merchant, 'the image of the black as presented for popular consumption' was nonetheless profoundly shaped by slavery in this period, 'both its imposition and the decades-long struggle against it' (p. 5). (Slavery was abolished in Britain in 1833, and British sailors subsequently patrolled the seas against the slave trade to other countries, notably the United

States and Brazil; p. 53.) Waters's research reveals that *Black Ey'd Susan* was preceded by abolitionist dramas of the late eighteenth and early nineteenth centuries, including one by Douglas Jerrold himself called *Descart, or the French Buccaneer* in 1828, just one year before his *Black Ey'd Susan* premiered. These popular spectacles, in which there was an 'almost reflexive yoking of Englishness, liberty and slavery' (p. 5), drew black characters as figures of pathos; in other words, in their pathetic situation and role, they provided the perfect opportunity for their white sailor saviours to prove their more advanced humanity. So, considered against the governing emotional precepts of melodrama, this story about a shark in the West Indies is not so out of place after all. But it also exposes some links between this hierarchy of feeling and an implicit yet consequential ideology of racial hierarchy.

The chain of hierarchy goes one step further into the realm of 'culture' where it positions 'high' culture above popular or 'low' culture. Waters describes the comic sketches of Charles Mathews, a famous English actor of the early nineteenth century whose one-person show *A Trip to America* (English Opera House, London, 1824) featured two caricatures of African Americans. One of these caricatures was an 'ignorant but self-important actor' who misspeaks the words of Shakespeare – in later versions he performs them in a gross 'black dialect' – and interpolates songs such as 'Opossum Up a Gum-Tree' into Hamlet's 'To be or not to be' soliloquy. The comedy of this sketch lies in 'the perceived incongruity of "black" and "high culture"' (p. 89); the actor's failed attempt at acting the lines of Shakespeare displays his racial inferiority, the incommensurability of a low human type associated more strongly with bodily nature than with abstracted (or poetic) mind and a high culture form linked precisely to abstraction and refinement, as we saw when considering the case of *Oedipus Rex*. Shakespeare's position at the pinnacle of English national culture and of high culture altogether, secured during the eighteenth century, was consolidated again in the nineteenth century in depictions such as Mathews's (Michael Dobson, *The Making of the National Poet*, 1992). In this way, then, Mathews's character crystallises the hierarchies of feeling, race, and cultural forms, where, in sum, emotion ranks over affect, human over animal, and mind over body, underpinning a hierarchy of cultural forms and sustaining a broader social – and culturally specific – hierarchy that elevates white over black and male over female, as we'll see shortly.

The value of melodrama

William's full and expressly white and male heroic humanity aside, some of the most active and intrinsically rewarding feeling moments of any play, and especially of a melodrama, are generated by and attached to the villain. He or she has the 'best' part – by which I mean the part that is most fun and interesting to portray – because the villain is the play's most active principal. Many a dramatic theorist has puzzled over the villain's appeal. German playwright Friedrich Schiller might have captured it most simply in his essay on 'The Pathetic' ([1793] 1974), in which he contends that action that 'testifies with energy to liberty, and to the force of the will' most fires the imagination (p. 466). By this logic, villains compel in the force or vitality of their actions rather than the moral direction of those actions. So melodrama's feeling-technologies with respect to plot and character are not engineered simply or solely to produce 'right' or 'morally appropriate' or 'socially acceptable' feeling in the audience. They produce feeling, period.

A number of the best commentators on the form, including Peter Brooks, Michael Booth, and Eric Bentley, contend that melodrama's appeal lies precisely in the clarity and abundance of its feeling. In *The Life of the Drama* (1965), Bentley suggests that melodrama represents the theatrical impulse itself, characterising melodrama as 'drama in its elemental form; it is the quintessence of drama' (p. 216). Brooks offers the freedom of emotional expression in melodrama as a key to its popularity, which is reminiscent of Schiller's assertion that representations of liberty are appealing. 'The desire to express all seems a fundamental characteristic of the melodramatic mode', Brooks observes, and this fullness of expression is meaningfully set against the common ethic of emotional repression for the sake of propriety (*The Melodramatic Imagination*, p. 4). In his defence of melodrama, James Rosenberg maintains that through its hyperbolic narratives, character portraits, and modes of physical and verbal expression, melodrama gives us a 'vicarious stimulation' of pure vitality, of life lived at its peak. 'There [onstage],' he writes, 'everything matters; every moment is significant; nothing is wasted; there, life *really* burns with a hard gemlike flame – as it so rarely does on the other side of the footlights' ('Melodrama', 1964, p. 178). In this comment lies another indicator of melodrama's appeal during the period of its emergence and efflorescence. Not only did it encourage feeling; it encouraged feeling among those whose workaday lives especially militated against feeling while nonetheless capitalising on their bodily labours: working-class industrial and domestic labourers. Melodrama drew back together in a pleasurable and positive way what had been forced apart by industrial labour practices, namely feeling and the body.

The theatres that specialised in spectacular fare such as nautical and gothic melodramas of the first half of the nineteenth century were largely of the minor theatre variety and were located in London's East End or on the Surrey (south) side of the Thames. As minor theatres, according to the terms of the Licensing Act of 1737, they were not allowed to present legitimate drama (that is, spoken drama), as that was the privilege of the Drury Lane, Covent Garden, and Haymarket theatres, those West End venues granted patents by King Charles II upon the Restoration of the monarchy (and theatres) in 1660. The minor houses (which, by the way, were decidedly major in their cultural impact and in the size of their auditoria and stages) evaded this restriction, in place until the Theatre Regulation Act of 1843, by innovating theatrical forms such as melodrama which relied on 'a combination of musical accompaniment and dumbshow to convey plot and meaning' (Booth, *Theatre in the Victorian Age*, 1991, p. 151). Nineteenth-century-theatre historian Michael Booth contextualises melodrama as follows: 'Of all 19th-century dramatic forms melodrama is the most indebted to music for mood, entrance and exit cues and leitmotifs to accompany its stock characters. The interpretation of emotion by means of gesture, bodily attitude and facial expression, long essential to tragic acting, became extended and habitual in melodrama, at first by legal necessity and then by custom' (p. 151).

It is noteworthy that a legal restriction on spoken dramatic expression produced a theatrical form that revelled in the fullness and even redundancy of expression. You might have noticed how the feeling-technologies of melodrama tend to pile up, one on top of the other, creating a surplus of expression and feeling by routing it through multiple channels. For instance, in the final scene of *Black Ey'd Susan*, William is to be hanged. The stage directions describe a meaningful tableau (a static stage-picture composed of characters and objects in expressive kinaesthetic relation): 'MASTER-AT-ARMS, *with a drawn sword under his arm, points next to the prisoner. –* WILLIAM, *without his neckcloth*' and surrounded by a phalanx of fellow sailors from all ranks (p. 136). This static picture indicating William's dire situation, as well as his preparedness for it, is completed by '*Music*'. Although the specifics of the music are not recorded in this passage, we might imagine how the strings and horns essential to any melodrama orchestra accompanied this scene. In their examination of 'Music in Melodrama', published in *Nineteenth Century Theatre & Film* (2002), Sarah Hibberd and Nanette Nielsen note that 'moments of high drama [such as this one] are usually effected by means of extremely simple musical devices … from horn triads to evoke the theme of hunting to diminished seventh-chords and tremolo strings to signify unease or fear' (p. 31). It is likely, then, that the music, through these simple devices, reinforced the solemnity of the occasion, offering the audience yet another medium to which they might respond emotively and in terms of sense perception; here, the music's appeal to the ear underscores quite literally the tableau's appeal to the eye.

The minor theatres' locations were also significant, positioned as they were in zones of industry such as Surrey and the East End, which attracted a variety of trade-related businesses and, with them, jobs for the growing working-class population of the area. In their analysis of census and repertoire data in *Reflecting the Audience: London Theatregoing, 1840–1880* (2001), Jim Davis and Victor Emeljanow paint a picture of the Surrey Theatre's local audience (it drew people from other parts of London as well, though in somewhat smaller numbers). The 1841 census records that the two dominant occupations in the area were domestic labour as servants (of whom there were 5,001, or 13.2 per cent of the area's population) and labourers (of whom there were 3,985, or 10.5 per cent of the population). Davis and Emeljanow state that 1861 census figures show a growing proportion of the population involved in domestic service and industrial labour (42.2 per cent and 35.1 per cent. respectively) (pp. 17–18). In the kitchens and factories, the shipyards and shops, Surrey-siders engaged in largely repetitive and alienated labours that stoked the engines of

England's nineteenth-century industrialisation. When patronising their local theatres, they were treated not merely to 'escapist fantasy', as some have characterised melodrama's entertainment value, but also to what we might imagine as a reclaiming of their bodies for something other than work. This claim was made through the ecstatic and multi-sensorial response to melodrama's multiform feeling-technologies.

Social value and social work

It is no coincidence that I've contrasted Sophocles' *Oedipus Rex* with Jerrold's *Black Ey'd Susan*. Not only is each exemplary of one of the two Horatian purposes for theatre – to profit (the mind) or to please (the body), respectively; their contrast also throws into sharp relief the different artistic and social values attached to each purpose. Speaking very generally now, those profitable forms are granted superior artistic and social value to pleasurable ones. Good melodramas may exist (indeed, they do), but 'good' in this formulation is often qualified as 'good *for a melodrama*'. In this usage, 'good' means exemplary of the form, but since the form itself is already considered to be degraded, a good melodrama can never be as good as a good tragedy, which carries greater cultural and aesthetic weight. As proof of melodrama's critical degradations, one need think only of colloquial uses of the word 'melodramatic' and its connotations of hyper-emotionality, narrative implausibility, and critical vacuity, as in the invective 'Don't be so melodramatic!' The absence of nineteenth-century theatre and most forms of popular entertainment from serious scholarly discussion in theatre studies until fairly recently (about the mid-twentieth century) is another sign of this hierarchy of value (Robertson Davies, *The Mirror of Nature*, 1983).

Two reasons help explain this hierarchy. First, as I've implied above, forms that profit, such as Greek tragedy, tend to downplay or redirect their affective influence on the spectator. They address the mind as though it has no physical extension, and the emotions represented in and activated by the plays tend to be the so-called cognitive emotions. In short, forms that profit are set in advanced developmental terrain. This is not to dismiss other factors that contribute to *Oedipus Rex*'s high art status – factors such as the noble class of the characters and the poetic dimensions of the text. Rather, it is to underscore the dubiously regarded place of feeling and its undeniably somatic – or embodied – dimension in theatre practice and studies. Frankly pleasurable forms such as melodrama, on the other hand, revel in their affecting effects in a quest to summon feeling responses and sensations of aliveness, in their activations of bodily sensation. This is where the cognitive science research into mirror neurons and mental images shows its larger value despite arguments over its limitations, as it demonstrates how the physical and mental properties of the brain/mind are connected; in their experiments that show how the brain lights up under different conditions, neuroscientists are demonstrating the physical aspect of thoughts and mental images. The biologist Changeux writes that mental pictures or 'representations are built up by the activation of neurons, whose dispersion throughout the multiple cortical areas determines the figurative or abstract character of the representation' (quoted in States, *The Pleasure of the Play*, p. 20).

Second, the hierarchy raising theatrical forms for profit above those for pleasure arises because forms that profit produce something to be taken away. In short, by making something that might be consumed – usually a lesson, an insight, or a value – theatres of profit are productive in a mode consonant with capitalist economy. (Note that this is the same economic system that structured the working lives of those who flocked to Surrey-side and East End theatres for their pleasurable entertainments; consider how the audience's pleasure might be redoubled at watching others work *for* them, for their entertainment.) As examples of a theatre of profit, take late nineteenth- and early twentieth-century 'problem plays' such as George Bernard Shaw's *Mrs Warren's Profession* (New Lyric Club, London, 1902), which staged debates about prostitution, and Sudermann's *Heimat*, in which Duse excelled in the role of an unwed mother. (Henrik Ibsen's plays, such as *A Doll's House* [Det Kongelige Teater, Copenhagen, 1879] and *Hedda Gabler* [Residenz-Theater, Munich, 1891], are also often lumped into the category of 'problem play' during this late-Victorian historical moment.) The problem play's profits would not be the transitory, personal, sometimes titillating ones of sensory and emotional arousal. Rather, the play might claim more durable, public, and serious value in the form of lessons to be taken away or issues for further discussion. As entertaining as *Mrs Warren's Profession* may have been in its wit and scandalous topicality, the play also elaborated a theory of the exploitation of women's labour in modern, capitalist society. (So already we see that theatres of profit are not necessarily allied with capitalist regimes; indeed, much of the modern history of profitable or socially beneficial theatre has been one of anti-capitalist sentiment; see Alan Read's *Theatre, Intimacy & Engagement*, 2008, and James Thompson's *Performance Affects*, 2009.)

Shaw, an admirer of Ibsen's innovations and a man of acute social and political conscience, expressed his intentions for *Mrs Warren's Profession* in typically clear-eyed fashion on the copy of the play submitted to the Lord Chamberlain, the licensor of plays for performance in London and Westminster, in 1898: 'This play is designed to give an extremely disagreeable, but much needed, shock to the conscience of the public in a matter of deep social importance' (quoted in L. W. Conolly, *'Mrs Warren's Profession* and the Lord Chamberlain', 2004, p. 50). It turned out that the Lord Chamberlain's office agreed with Shaw – but only on the point that the play was extremely disagreeable. In fact, *Mrs Warren's Profession* was deemed so reprehensible in its subject matter that the Lord Chamberlain's office prevented the professional production of the unexpurgated text until 1925. Shaw's 'effective instrument of moral propaganda', as he calls the play in his printed preface to its 1930 publication, was produced instead in 1902 by a private company – and hence not subject to the licensing restrictions (in effect until 1968) – the Stage Society, which included among its members Harley Granville-Barker and J. M. Barrie. It would seem that *Mrs Warren's Profession* overshot the mark of being socially valuable, or that it performed its social work in too explicit a way to be easily digested. Its didactic intent, however, is not in doubt.

On the other hand, popular entertainments such as melodrama, vaudeville, minstrelsy, music hall, musical theatre, and street performance are precisely, evidently, and expressly non-productive in this way. If we follow Peggy Phelan's argument that performance's ontology is disappearance, popular entertainments are the ground zero of performance; they leave nothing to take away. Let me nuance that claim slightly: they leave nothing *new* to take away, no fresh insight or uncommon lesson. Certainly melodrama has its lessons: that good will be rewarded and vice punished, that marriage is sacred, that good will out. But these lessons are not revelatory; rather, they confirm *at the level of feeling* the dominant moral ethos of the culture. In other words, they are recycled and, therefore, reassuring.

Let's take a different example to illuminate the 'anti-profit' motive of much popular entertainment done expressly for pleasure. (Here, we're drawing together two connotations of the word 'profit': the Horatian sense of 'benefit' and the capitalist sense of 'financial gain, return or surplus'.) Consider the magician and his or her act. The ways in which the magician manipulates objects arguably overturns the ways in which workers in factories, for instance, were meant to manipulate objects, thereby reversing the dominant codes of production in Western capitalist society. Industrial workers turned bits of wood and metal into widgets for sale; they made something new. The magician, too, manipulates stuff (rabbits, hats, rings), but without making anything of it. The 'work' of prestidigitation yields no 'products': the rabbit generally disappears again after being pulled from the hat; the rings link and unlink in endless succession across performances (Paul Bouissac, *Circus and Culture*, 1976). In addition, magic tricks often toy with our senses; they play with and stimulate our bodies in that way. Sleight-of-hand manoeuvres, as when a coin magically appears from behind an audience member's ear only to disappear again from the magician's hand, trick our sense of sight – and our expectations.

In a way similar to the circus magician, street performers in New York City's Washington Square Park have an ambivalent relationship to authorised models of production. They, too, produce no removable object in their juggling, comedy, and mime acts. In addition, they perform this enjoyable non-production in a public venue (the park), for free (if one doesn't want to or can't contribute), and on their own schedule (though in accordance with peak foot traffic at the site). The signs of their not-working status are littered around them, denoted by the environment in which they perform, which is a space of leisure, and by their costuming: they can't look as though they make too much money, as that would reduce one incentive passers-by have to toss a couple of coins in the hat. In *Drawing a Circle in the Square* (1990), performance scholar Sally Harrison-Pepper observes of street performers that they can't be 'too "smooth." They must communicate messages about money and professionalism that are fundamentally different than those of the indoor performer' (p. 16). Their non-professional and not-working status is also written into law and policing practices. Harrison-Pepper documents the arrests of street performers in San Francisco, where street performance is illegal; they were taken in for 'willfully and maliciously blocking the street' (p. 29). In a 1983 *New York Times* article cited by Harrison-Pepper, a Chicago police lieutenant testifies to what he perceives as the fine line between a street performer and a mendicant (p. 32). Such is the legally precarious feeling-labour of some popular entertainers. Its public service, if you will, goes unrecognised as such, just as melodrama's often did and still usually does.

Profiting from feeling-work

This odd meeting of Oedipus and Mrs Warren on the side of profit is propitious as both train our eyes on the relation between the place of the body, its evidence, knowledge, and labours, and the way in which critical and social value is frequently determined in the Western theatrical tradition. In both cases, the physical body (Oedipus' swollen foot – as well as other possible physical evidence of his blood relationship to Jocasta and Laius – and Mrs Warren's sex workers) is sublimated – by the tragic form in the first instance and by the Lord Chamberlain's censorship in the second. (Shaw produced an expurgated version that changed the title character's profession from madam to shoplifter in order to establish his legal performance rights to the play following its publication in 1898; the Lord Chamberlain's reader promptly licensed that version – see Conolly, '*Mrs Warren's*

Profession and the Lord Chamberlain'.) The meeting is propitious in another sense, too, because the prostitute, as dramatic figure, functions as a kind of anti-Oedipus; where his nobility requires that he transcend the physical, she is required by her lowly profession to act on her bodily knowledge and solicit proofs of the body's physical excitations. As such, this character who provides sensory and emotional satisfactions to her clients via her body is an important one for our story of theatre and feeling. She effectively encapsulates the relations among affect/emotion, status, and value articulated above. Now we'll add gender back into the mix (I hinted at it earlier in my discussion of Tom the sailor and the bumboat woman). Above I drew an analogy between *theatrical representation* and brain function; here, the analogy is between *theatrical labour* and prostitution. The link is their embodied, emotional work.

The prostitute is an age-old metaphor for the actress, one that theatre scholar Kirsten Pullen traces to the Greek 'flute girls', or *auletrides*, who entertained and then sexually gratified the hosts of the *symposia* as early as the fifth century BCE, the same century that witnessed the golden age of Greek tragedy (see Pullen's 'Actresses', 2006, and her *Actresses and Whores*, 2005). Professional actresses, including those of the Renaissance Italian popular form *commedia dell'arte*, the early modern French theatre, the English Restoration stage, and pre-twentieth-century Chinese theatre, were commonly falsely accused of being prostitutes on the basis of the similar features of some aspects of the work of actresses and prostitutes. Both the actress and the prostitute set their bodies out for public display and consumption, for which they were paid, for instance. Gilli Bush-Bailey observes the common and presumptuous elision between the actress's public and private identities, 'the visual spectacle of her acting body *on* stage and the availability of her sexually active body *off* stage', in her contribution to *The Cambridge Companion to the Actress* (2007, p. 15). Tracy C. Davis, whose *Actresses as Working Women: Their Social Identity in Victorian Culture* (1991) is a landmark of feminist scholarship on the working conditions and cultural meanings of the nineteenth-century English actress, remarks that not only were actresses remunerated for their public display (and thus, practically and metaphorically, for selling their bodies) but, as financially independent women workers, they also transgressed bourgeois expectations of women's 'appropriate' behaviour in other ways (pp. 69–101). The label 'prostitute' thus negatively marked actresses' gender exceptionalism as much as it slurred their affecting emotional and physical labour – in other words, their acting.

Gypsy (Broadway Theatre, New York, 1959), the musical retelling of the rise to burlesque stardom of the stripper Gypsy Rose Lee by Jules Styne, Stephen Sondheim, and Arthur Laurents, is a telling example of the semantic slippage and functional overlap between the actress and the sex worker in the domain of theatre. The story of Louise crystallises this dynamic. At the outset of her career as a child performer in vaudeville, Louise is the lesser half of a sister act; she memorably plays the rear end of a cow in one of their numbers. Their signature act is a song and dance piece that recurs throughout the show as a leitmotif: 'Let Me Entertain You'. In its first iteration, when the sisters are young children, the song is performed as a sprightly waltz professing the child performer's (cute) desire to please by being entertaining. Later, when 'Let Me Entertain You' is enfolded into an act called 'Baby June [Louise's older sister] and Her Newsboys' (Louise plays the decidedly unglamorous role of a newsboy), the song goes more up tempo, but June's forthright and vocally forceful presentation of its lyrics preserves its naïveté. In Act 2, after June has eloped and left Louise alone with their overbearing stage mother, Rose, Louise is accidentally thrust into the spotlight as the replacement headliner at a Wichita burlesque house. In this new context, 'Let Me Entertain You' really swings. It assumes its full affective, sexual significance, a significance that has been latent since its first rendition but, under the lights of the burlesque stage, is now explicit. 'And if you're real good, I'll make you feel good. I want your spirits to climb. So, let me entertain you and we'll have a real good time, yes sir! We'll have a real good time.' This turn also illuminates anew the conditions of live theatrical performance, especially for women and, now in hindsight at play's end, for girls. For all its wonderful show tunes and star turns, which produce some of musical theatre's richest pleasures, *Gypsy* is a sceptical (if not exactly cynical) look at the feeling-labours required especially of female talent, a talent pool always already associated with bodily pleasures and feeling-labour because of its gender. One might say that *Gypsy* lays bare a theatrical service economy in which female performers are the primary feeling-technology.

Moreover, Louise's story, which transpires over a period of some years spent on the road searching for fortune and fame, highlights the kind of repetitive, not always fulfilling yet personally and emotionally taxing labour that is so many actors' experience of theatre work. Hers is the story of an 'overnight sensation' a long time in the making. Listened to in a different way, with an emphasis on its first two words, 'Let Me Entertain You' can sound like an audition plea.

Feeling's professional significance: acting

I proposed just above that *Gypsy* exposes a theatrical service economy in which female performers are the primary feeling-technology; it is they who raise spirits. But what are the feeling-technologies for actors? By what means do they raise spirits, play sentiment, transmit rapture? This question has plagued actors, directors, teachers, and theorists since time immemorial. Theatre historian and performance theorist Joseph Roach masterfully charts a history of answers to this question from the seventeenth to the mid-twentieth century in *The Player's Passion: Studies in the Science of Acting* (1985). He brings to the fore the scientific theories of body and mind that underlay methods of acting. These range from the idea from Galenic philosophy (*c*.131–*c*.201 CE) that the body might be literally inspired by ethereal spirits, to the notion of the body as a clock in Denis Diderot's musings from the seventeenth century, to the principle of the body as a bundle of trainable reflexes, following the research of Russian physiologist Ivan Pavlov during the twentieth. The current emphasis in theatre studies on cognitive science, neurobiology, and mirror neurons comes from yet another psychobiological paradigm of the human body/mind (see Bruce McConachie, *Engaging Audiences*, 2008, and McConachie and F. Elizabeth Hart, *Performance and Cognition*, 2006) and must be historicised as such. In this final section of *Theatre & Feeling*, I reflect briefly on feeling and its feeling-labours as what Roach identifies as a 'question of daily professional significance to the actor' (p. 13). This will serve as my last proof for feeling's necessity to theatre. We've seen already how feeling structures and enables the theatrical experience on both sides of the footlights, providing theatre with its *raison d'être*, its purpose, and its value. In what follows, we'll take a quick look at how feeling – and doing things with feeling – informs much contemporary actor training and performance and influences how actors are perceived.

The focus on actors over other theatre workers (designers, directors, technicians, critics) makes sense because their profession as it has developed in dominant theatrical practice in the twentieth-century West associates them with the feeling body in a way that cannot be ignored. The actor's involvement with the body is primary – both inasmuch as her body is her instrument and enabler of her working life and because her job is to activate the feeling bodies of audience members via their systems of sense perception and emotional repertoires. Acting is also the theatre profession in which devotion to and training of the body as a whole system encompassing body and mind is essential. In text-based performance, for instance, one often passes from reading the play to putting bits of it on its feet to analysis and back again, thereby drawing together cognitive and bodily knowledge. This professionally mandated emphasis on the body is not only evident in its most obvious outcomes – that is, in terms of physical appearance, as in the suspiciously high rate of plastic surgery, especially among film and television actors. It is also apparent in the kind of psycho-physical training professional actors undergo – and keep up with – to stay in form. I'm thinking here of the vocal exercises and physical warm-ups with which most actors precede performance – exercises that prepare the actor's body for its onstage exertions of vocal projection and modulation, physical activity, and gestural precision. Stories such as that of Hugh Jackman, whose preparation for the role of Australian singer Peter Allen in the Broadway musical *The Boy from Oz* (Imperial Theatre, New York, 2003–4) included song and dance rehearsals and twice-weekly vitamin shots, also come to mind, as do the panoply of exercises that assist actors in 'getting into character', in calibrating their emotional repertoires with those experienced by the character or demanded by the form night after night.

Interestingly, and consistent again with the actors-as-prostitutes analogy, actors are sometimes admonished for getting too 'cerebral'. Several have traced this concern with over-thinking by actors to the precepts of Russian theatre actor, director, and champion of realist acting technique Constantin Stanislavsky. With Vladimir Nemirovitch-Danchenko, Stanislavsky co-founded in 1896 the Moscow

Art Theatre, where Anton Chekhov's plays received their first stagings. Most salient for our purposes is the fact that Stanislavsky developed an approach to acting that enabled actors reliably and repeatedly to produce emotions (and not just emotional displays) on stage. It was not enough for Stanislavsky that actors replicate the external signs of emotion in codified displays, as did their immediate precursors in the melodramatic theatre. Rather, as explained in Stanislavsky's *An Actor Prepares* (1936), they were enjoined to enter the inner life of a character by transferring analogous feelings from their own experience to the part. He described the actor's goal as 'the creation of [the] inner life of a human spirit, and its expression in artistic form' (p. 14).

To do this, the actor was taken through a series of exercises that would help her reach the subconscious 'through conscious means' (*An Actor Prepares*, p. 166). Stanislavsky writes, 'You can understand a part, sympathize with the person portrayed, and put yourself in his place, so that you will act as he would. That will arouse feelings in the actor that are *analogous* to those required for the part. But those feelings will belong, not to the person created by the author of the play, but to the actor himself' (p. 167, emphasis in original). In *Stanislavsky in Focus* (2009), Sharon Carnicke describes a number of means on which Stanislavsky depended to arouse feelings for use in character portrayal. Following Stanislavsky's usage, Carnicke calls these ' "lures" to incite the actor's memory of emotion', and they include: stage environments (sets, lighting) and props; psycho-physical techniques such as relaxation, concentration; sparks to the imagination such as mining personal associations with the play; and examination of the playtext itself (pp. 126–27). In his own directing, Stanislavsky had a penchant for soundscapes for productions. Chekhov disliked hearing birds chirping, water burbling, and crickets buzzing in the outdoor scenes of his play *The Seagull* (Alexandrinsky Theatre, Moscow, 1896; Moscow Art Theatre, 1898), for instance, thinking these details overly concerned with reproducing external realities and therefore distracting from the internal realities of the characters. He reportedly commented, 'I shall write a new play and it will begin with a character saying, "How wonderfully quiet it is! There are no birds to be heard, no dogs, no cuckoos, no owls, no nightingales, no clocks, no harness bells, and not a single cricket"' (quoted in Edward Braun, *The Director and the Stage*, 1982, p. 73). For Stanislavsky, however, these soundscapes were effective lures to tap the emotional life of actors; they acted as stimuli to which the actors' feeling systems would respond. Moreover, these sound cues helped create mood, which, as you remember from above, would dispose actors to certain types of feeling response appropriate to the moment and character. Stanislavsky says of this in *An Actor Prepares*, 'When the external production of a play … meets the needs of the play and produces the right mood it helps the actor to formulate the inner aspect of his role, it influences his whole psychic state and capacity to feel. Under such conditions the setting is a definite stimulus to our emotion' (p. 170).

This, then, is one feeling-technology promoted by Stanislavsky – using conscious means such as low light, the plaintive sound of bird calls, and an over-tight costume to solicit a feeling response of sad discomfort in the actor. The actor's feeling of discomfort may principally be the result of the ill-fitting costume – that is the actor's emotion – but it is analogous to the character's sense of, say, feeling out of place called for by the script and its analysis. Through lures such as sound, lighting, and script – all used as stimuli to feeling response – actors may project themselves into the circumstances in which the character is immersed; this, in turn, will elicit emotions appropriate to the character, real to and really experienced by the actor (though, again, in analogical form), and persuasive to the audience.

The more famous – because more contested – feeling-technology developed in the early years of Stanislavsky's forty-year career in the theatre is that called 'emotion memory'. Where the stage environment functions as a set of external stimuli to feeling response in the actor, emotion memory acts as an inner stimulus to emotion. Emotion memory in Stanislavsky's formulation is the ability to recall vividly the feelings summoned by past experiences in such a way that one relives those emotional sensations. Importantly, however, Stanislavsky does not advise actors to use personal memory directly; rather, he perceives emotion memory as 'a kind of synthesis of memory on a large scale. It is purer, more condensed, compact, substantial and sharper than the actual happenings' (p. 163). In other words, the emotion memory to which an actor returns to infuse life into a role is not a specific, individual memory but a memory of emotion transmuted by time, connected to other like emotion memories, and distributed across individuals. By the distribution of emotion memory I mean that the storehouse of emotion memory is not only built out of one's personal reserve of affective experience but also drawn from the vicarious experience of others. Stanislavsky therefore encourages building up one's emotional memory reserves by acquiring 'material from life around you, real and imaginary, from reminiscences, books, art, science, knowledge of all kinds, from journeys, museums and above all from communication with other human beings' (p. 180). One's inner stimulus, then, often comes from outside.

Stanislavsky's early emphasis on the emotional aspects of acting, on helping actors get into character and respond to the play's circumstances as if they were the character, was revolutionary at the time and has since earned him a legacy of no small importance. One can trace his influence to the American Method school of acting (typified by Marlon Brando and Dustin Hoffman, for instance) and its effects on most acting programmes in the West today. However, as theatre scholars and directors Sharon Carnicke and Rhonda Blair have explained, it has also led to an overemphasis on the affective aspects of Stanislavsky's system, and especially on the emotion memory feeling-technology. Carnicke attributes this distortion to Lee Strasberg, founder of the Method, who out of Stanislavsky's repertoire of feeling-technologies and lures to emotion honed in on what he called 'affective memory' and developed a number of techniques for drawing out emotion. Carnicke writes, 'In responding to Stanislavsky's vision of the unconscious as a large house with many places in which to hide a precious jeweled "bead" of emotion, Strasberg explains that, in his opinion finding this bead is the actor's "true task." Moreover, he states, "this was the task I was to devote myself to in establishing the Method"' (*Stanislavsky in Focus*, p. 128). In 'Reconsidering Stanislavsky' (2002), Blair concludes that some theatre practitioners, under the influence of the Strasberg Method or its variants, 'justify a decontextualized, hyperpersonalized emotionalism or narcissism' (p. 179).

This accent on actorly emotionalism – on summoning and displaying repeatedly, sincerely, and convincingly real emotions for consumption by paying audiences – is condensed in catchphrases encouraging actors to prioritise their emotional body/mind over their thinking body/mind. Blair, who has begun an important reconsideration of the Stanislavsky system and its derivatives from the point of view of cognitive science insights into the 'emotional brain' (most extensively in her 2008 book *The Actor, Image, and Action*), writes of this phenomenon, '"Get out of your head" is a phrase used by many acting teachers as a way to admonish actors to be more present to the moment in a scene or a play' ('Reconsidering Stanislavsky', p. 188). Thus, the caution towards the feeling body that I've noted in preceding examples – where high cultural status is secured in part through a distancing from or repression of the somatic, and where affective excess is the signature of a 'backwards' or less-than-fully-human population, for instance – is thrown to the wind in the example of the actor. The actor's theatrical value is relegated expressly to the bodily in a way that can be degrading for its perceived distance from the more culturally valued arena of thought. This returns us to one risk of feeling-work – that it can go un- or undervalued because of its negative associations.

Conclusion

And yet, for all its risks, the feeling-work of theatre offers real and substantial rewards to those who do it and to those who watch it. It allows for and offers vicarious experience: the experience of someone else experiencing something. As we've learned, witnessing another's actions and emotional experiences can create the same neurological imprint as doing or feeling them oneself. In this way, vicarious experience is very intimate indeed. In its intimacy, the vicarious experience of experience on which much performance is based is offered as the theatre's 'good', both in the sense of its social gift and in the sense of its consumable object. In his most recent book, *It* (2007), Joseph Roach provocatively recasts the history of theatre in terms of the good of what he calls 'synthetic experience', a cognate to vicarious experience. The theatre is a port of entry into another's life and another kind of living. It is, then, the vivifying aspect of vicarious experience offered by the feeling-labours of theatre workers that makes it theatre's good (or benefit). However, as Roach is quick to point out, theatre's good is also a consumer good, a thing – or, more aptly, a service – to be bought and sold. 'That people would part with good money to experience experience (by vicariously living through someone else's embodiment of it) was a discovery as exciting to some as fire,' he observes (p. 29). It is in this context of use that my use of 'feeling-labour' and 'feeling-technologies' resonates most strongly and points us once again to the centrality of feeling in all its types to the 'very dynamic and labile' service that is the theatre (p. 29).

Feeling is the core of the theatre. It furnishes theatre's reason for being, cements its purpose – whether such purpose is construed as entertainment or instruction – and undergirds the art form's social work and value. Moreover, it organises theatre's functions and theatre people's professional lives. And finally, it attracts audiences. Roach connects the theatre's attractions to a basic human need, suggesting that 'synthetic experience must answer the human need, regulated by both curiosity and fear, to experience life vicariously as well as directly' (p. 28). We attend the theatre to feel *more*, even if it doesn't make us feel *better*; we go to have our emotional life acknowledged and patterned, managed into coherent storylines, and exposed in all its tumult (or its banality). We go to experience an expanded, more expressive, and nuanced range of feeling imaginatively and viscerally with the aid of another person or agency. We go, in the end, because feeling matters.

further reading

The theatre and its workers have addressed the topic of feeling, at least implicitly, for a long time now, so a list of further reading on the subject could reasonably get quite lengthy. Almost any reflection on acting or spectatorship/reception will run up against feeling. Judith Lynn Hanna's *The Performer-Audience Connection* (1983), for example, analyses post-show survey data and interviews with dancers on the subject of what they felt during the performance. I offer here, then, those sources that have most nourished my thinking on the subject to date, some sources that are representative of a position or turn with respect to theatre or feeling, and some that are not included in the book as a result of its focus on Western theatrical traditions.

Studies in theatrical feeling organise themselves around two related but distinct poles: the affective turn and the cognitive turn. In the former category, the publications below by Brian Massumi, Sara Ahmed, Heather Love, and the late Eve Kosofsky Sedgwick and the collection edited by Patricia Ticineto Clough have been constitutive. Within theatre and performance studies, Nicholas Ridout's *Stage Fright, Animals and Other Theatrical Problems*, Joseph Roach's *The Player's Passion*, Jill Dolan's *Utopia in Performance*, and José Esteban Muñoz's influential *Theatre Journal* article 'Feeling Brown' have in many respects laid the groundwork for more express and sustained thinking on feeling. Dolan's 2004 special issue of *Modern Drama* collects a sample of other scholars' work invested in thinking feeling, and there is fascinating work forthcoming from Ridout again, Rebecca Schneider, and Sara Warner, in addition to what they've already published. Peta Tait's *Performing Emotions* addresses Stanislavsky's theatre and approach to emotion, though drawing on a wider range of theories of emotion. In his *Engaging Audiences*, Bruce McConachie argues the advantages of the cognitive turn in theatre studies, outlining an approach to reception theory that draws on neuroscience models; the volume edited by McConachie and F. Elizabeth Hart maps the area. Rhonda Blair's *The Actor, Image, and Action* addresses the other side of the coin – acting – from a similarly cognitive-science-based model of mind/body; earlier introductions of neuroscience into acting theory include Susana Bloch, Pedro Orthous, and Guy Santibañez-H's contribution to Phillip B. Zarrilli's *Acting (Re)considered*. John Emigh's pioneering interest in this area and its cross-cultural resonances is outlined in his 'Performance Studies, Neuroscience, and the Limits of Culture'.

Useful general introductions to the study of emotion include Dylan Evans's *Emotion: The Science of Sentiment* (which, it should be noted, tends towards evolutionary biologism) and Keith Oatley's *Emotions: A Brief History*, approached through the field of psychology.

Finally, some titles listed here are not mentioned in the text but would have been had the book been longer and the author more nimble. The treatise *Fushikaden* (Teachings on Style and the Flower) by the fifteenth-century Japanese Noh theatre master Zeami considers in some detail the role of emotion for the actor and for the audience. Indian sage Bharata Muni's *Natya Sastra* (which is very difficult to date with any certainty but which scholars tend to place in the second or third century CE) identifies eight key emotions, their physical displays, and their emotional effect on audiences. Contemporary directors and devisers Anne Bogart, Tadashi Suzuki, Phillip Zarrilli, and Richard Schechner, to name only a few of those most visible and active in the West, have developed their own psycho-physical approaches to performance based on Zeami's or Bharata's principles. Representative published works by them are listed below.

Abrams, M. H. *The Mirror and the Lamp: Romantic Theory and the Critical Tradition*. New York: Oxford UP, 1953.

Ahmed, Sara. *The Cultural Politics of Emotion*. Edinburgh: Edinburgh UP, 2004.

Albrecht, Ernest. *The Contemporary Circus: Art of the Spectacular*. Lanham, MD: Scarecrow, 2006.

Aristotle. *The Poetics*. Trans. S. H. Butcher. Intro. Francis Fergusson. New York: Hill & Wang, 1961.

Artaud, Antonin. *The Theatre and Its Double*. New York: Grove, 1958.

Baker, George Pierce. *Dramatic Technique*. Boston, MA: Houghton Mifflin, 1919.

Barish, Jonas. *The Anti-theatrical Prejudice*. Berkeley: U of California P, 1981.

Bennett, Susan. 'Theatre Audiences, Redux.' *Theatre Survey* 47.2 (2006): 225–30.

Bentley, Eric. *The Life of the Drama*. London: Methuen, 1965.

Bharata. *The Natya Sastra of Bharatamuni*. Trans. into English by a board of scholars. Delhi, India: Sri Satguru, 1987.

Blair, Rhonda. 'Reconsidering Stanislavsky: Feeling, Feminism, and the Actor.' *Theatre Topics* 12.2 (2002): 177–90.

————. *The Actor, Image, and Action: Acting and Cognitive Neuroscience*. New York: Routledge, 2008.

Bloch, Susana, Pedro Orthous, and Guy Santibañez-H. 'Effector Patterns of Basic Emotions: A Psychophysiological Method for Training Actors.' *Acting (Re)considered: Theories and Practices*. Ed. Phillip B. Zarrilli. New York: Routledge, 1995. 197–218.

Bogart, Anne. *A Director Prepares: Seven Essays on Art and Theatre*. New York: Routledge, 2001.

Booth, Michael R. *Theatre in the Victorian Age*. Cambridge: Cambridge UP, 1991.

Boucicault, Dion. 'Illusions of the Stage.' *Scientific American* suppl. X, 1881: 4265–66.

Bouissac, Paul. *Circus and Culture: A Semiotic Approach*. Bloomington: Indiana UP, 1976.

Braun, Edward, ed. *The Director and the Stage: From Naturalism to Grotowski*. New York: Holmes & Meier, 1982.

Brook, Peter. *The Empty Space*. New York: Atheneum, 1968.

Brooks, Peter. *The Melodramatic Imagination: Balzac, Henry James, Melodrama, and the Mode of Excess*. New Haven, CT: Yale UP, 1976.

Bush-Bailey, Gilli. 'Revolution, Legislation and Autonomy.' *The Cambridge Companion to the Actress*. Ed. Maggie B. Gale and John Stokes. Cambridge: Cambridge UP, 2007. 15–32.

Carnicke, Sharon M. *Stanislavsky in Focus: An Acting Master for the Twenty-First Century*. 2nd ed. New York: Routledge, 2009.

Clough, Patricia Ticineto, ed., with Jean Halley. *The Affective Turn: Theorizing the Social*. Durham, NC: Duke UP, 2007.

Conolly, L. W. '*Mrs Warren's Profession* and the Lord Chamberlain.' *SHAW: The Annual of Bernard Shaw Studies* 24 (2004): 46–95.

Darwin, Charles. *The Expression of the Emotions in Man and Animals*. London: J. Murray, 1872.

Davies, Robertson. *The Mirror of Nature*. The Alexander Lectures 1982. Toronto: U of Toronto P, 1983.

Davis, Jim, and Victor Emeljanow. *Reflecting the Audience: London Theatregoing, 1840–1880*. Iowa City: U of Iowa P, 2001.

Davis, Tracy C. *Actresses as Working Women: Their Social Identity in Victorian Culture*. Gender and Performance series. Gen. eds. Tracy C. Davis and Susan Bassnett. London and New York: Routledge, 1991.

Disher, Maurice Willson. *Blood and Thunder: Mid-Victorian Melodrama and Its Origins*. London: Muller, 1949.

Dobson, Michael. *The Making of the National Poet: Shakespeare, Adaptation, and Authorship, 1660–1769*. Oxford: Oxford UP, 1992.

Dolan, Jill, ed. *Utopian Performatives*. Spec. iss. of *Modern Drama* 47.2 (2004).

———. *Utopia in Performance: Finding Hope at the Theater*. Ann Arbor: U of Michigan P, 2005.

Durkheim, Emile. 'The Dualism of Human Nature and Its Social Conditions.' Trans. C. Blend. *Essays on Sociology and Philosophy*. Ed. K. H. Wolff. New York: Harper Torchbooks, 1964. 325–40.

Ekman, Paul. 'Expression and the Nature of Emotion.' *Approaches to Emotion*. Ed. K. Scherer and P. Ekman. Hillsdale, NJ: Lawrence Erlbaum, 1984. 319–44.

Eliot, Lise. *Pink Brain, Blue Brain: How Small Differences Grow into Troublesome Gaps — and What We Can Do about It*. Boston, MA: Houghton Mifflin Harcourt, 2009.

Emigh, John. 'Performance Studies, Neuroscience, and the Limits of Culture.' *Teaching Performance Studies*. Ed. Nathan Stucky and Cynthia Wimmer. Carbondale: Southern Illinois UP, 2002. 261–78.

Evans, Dylan. *Emotion: The Science of Sentiment*. Oxford: Oxford UP, 2001.

Gallese, Vittorio, Luciano Fadiga, Leonardo Fogassi, and Giacomo Rizzolatti. 'Action Recognition in the Premotor Cortex.' *Brain* 119 (1996): 593–609.

Gallese, Vittorio, Christian Keysers, and Giacomo Rizzolatti. 'A Unifying View of the Basis of Social Cognition.' *TRENDS in Cognitive Science* 8.9 (2004): 396–403.

Garner, Stanton B., Jr. *Bodied Spaces: Phenomenology and Performance in Contemporary Drama*. Ithaca, NY: Cornell UP, 1994.

Gergely, György, and Gergely Cisbra. 'The Social Construction of the Cultural Mind: Imitative Learning as a Mechanism of Human

Pedagogy.' Contribution of Mirroring Processes to Human Mindreading/La Contribution des Processus de Résonance à la Cognition Sociale. International workshop, 8–11 December 2005, Château de Maffliers, France. 23 October 2009 <http:// mirrorneurons.free.fr/Gergely_&_Csibra_2005_IS.pdf>.

Hanna, Judith Lynn. *The Performer-Audience Connection: Emotion to Metaphor in Dance and Society*. Austin: U of Texas P, 1983.

Harrison-Pepper, Sally. *Drawing a Circle in the Square: Street Performing in New York's Washington Square Park*. Jackson: UP of Mississippi, 1990.

Hart, Moss. *Act One: An Autobiography*. New York: St. Martin's, 1989.

Hibberd, Sarah, and Nanette Nielsen. 'Music in Melodrama: "The Burden of Ineffable Expression"?' *Nineteenth Century Theatre & Film* 29.2 (2002): 30–39.

Hochschild, Arlie. *The Managed Heart: Commercialization of Human Feeling* [1983]. 20th Anniversary Ed. Berkeley: U of California P, 2003.

James, Louis. 'Taking Melodrama Seriously: Theatre and Nineteenth-Century Studies.' *History Workshop* 3.1 (1977): 151–58.

James, William. 'What Is an Emotion?' *Mind* 9 (1884): 188–205.

Jerrold, Douglas. *Black Ey'd Susan. Nineteenth-Century British Drama: An Anthology of Representative Plays*. Ed. Leonard R. N. Ashley. Lanham, MD: UP of America, 1989. 102–37.

Kandinsky, Wassily, and Franz Marc, eds. *The Blaue Reiter Almanac* [1912]. Ed. and intro. Klaus Lankheit. Trans. Henning Falkenstein, with the assistance of Manug Terzian and Gertrude Hinderlie. New York: Viking, 1974.

Love, Heather. *Feeling Backward: Loss and the Politics of Queer History*. Cambridge, MA: Harvard UP, 2007.

Massumi, Brian. *Parables for the Virtual: Movement, Affect, Sensation*. Durham, NC, and London: Duke UP, 2002.

McConachie, Bruce. *Engaging Audiences: A Cognitive Approach to Spectating in the Theatre*. New York: Palgrave Macmillan, 2008.

McConachie, Bruce, and F. Elizabeth Hart, eds. *Performance and Cognition: Theatre Studies and the Cognitive Turn*. New York: Routledge, 2006.

Miller, Arthur. *Death of a Salesman*. New York: Viking, 1949.

Muñoz, José Esteban. 'Feeling Brown: Ethnicity and Affect in Ricardo Bracho's *The Sweetest Hangover (and Other STDs)*.' *Theatre Journal* 52.1 (2000): 67–79.

Muñoz, José Esteban. *Cruising Utopia: The Politics and Performance of Queer Futurity*. New York: New York UP, 2009.

Oatley, Keith. *Emotions: A Brief History*. Oxford: Blackwell, 2004.

Pelletier, Pol. *Joy*. Trans. Linda Gaboriau. *Anthology of Québec Women's Plays in English Translation, Volume 2 (1987–2003)*. Ed. Louise H. Forsyth. Toronto: Playwrights Canada Press, 2008. 125–71.

Percival, John. *Theatre in My Blood: A Biography of John Cranko*. London: Herbert, 1983.

Phelan, Peggy. *Unmarked: The Politics of Performance*. New York: Routledge, 1993.

Pullen, Kirsten. *Actresses and Whores: On Stage and in Society*. Cambridge: Cambridge UP, 2005.

————. 'Actresses.' *Encyclopedia of Prostitution and Sex Work*. Ed. Melissa Hope Ditmore. Westport, CT: Greenwood, 2006. 9–11.

Read, Alan. *Theatre, Intimacy & Engagement: The Last Human Venue*. Basingstoke, UK, and New York: Palgrave Macmillan, 2008.

Ridout, Nicholas. *Stage Fright, Animals and Other Theatrical Problems*. Cambridge: Cambridge UP, 2007.

Roach, Joseph. *The Player's Passion: Studies in the Science of Acting*. London and Toronto: Associated UP; Newark: U of Delaware P, 1985.

————. *It*. Ann Arbor: U of Michigan P, 2007.

Rosenberg, James L. 'Melodrama.' *The Context and Craft of Drama: Critical Essays on the Nature of Drama and Theatre*. Ed. Robert W. Corrigan and James L. Rosenberg. San Francisco: Chandler, 1964. 168–85.

Saxe, Rebecca. 'Against Simulation: The Argument from Error.' *TRENDS in Cognitive Science* 9.4 (2005): 174–79.

Schechner, Richard. 'Rasaesthetics.' *TDR* 45.3 (2001): 27–50.

Schiller, Friedrich von. 'The Pathetic' [1793]. *Dramatic Theory and Criticism: Greeks to Grotowski*. Ed. Bernard F. Dukore. New York: Holt, Rinehart and Winston, 1974. 458–67.

Sedgwick, Eve Kosofsky. *Touching Feeling: Affect, Pedagogy, Performativity*. Durham, NC: Duke UP, 2003.

Shaw, George Bernard. *Our Theatres in the Nineties. Collected Works*. Ed. Ayot St Lawrence. New York: W.H. Wise, 1931. Vol. 3.

————. *Mrs Warren's Profession. Plays Unpleasant*. New York: Penguin, 1986. 213–86.

Sophocles. *Oedipus the King*. Trans. David Grene. *Sophocles I*. Ed. David
    Grene and Richmond Lattimore. Chicago, IL, and London: U of
    Chicago P, 1954. 9–76.

Stanislavsky, Constantin. 'Emotion Memory.' *An Actor Prepares*. Trans.
    Elizabeth Reynolds Hapgood. New York: Theatre Arts Books, 1936.
    154–81.

———. 'Imagination.' *An Actor Prepares*. Trans. Elizabeth Reynolds
    Hapgood. New York: Theatre Arts Books, 1936. 54–71.

States, Bert O. *The Pleasure of the Play*. Ithaca, NY: Cornell UP,
    1994.

Styne, Jules, Stephen Sondheim, and Arthur Laurents. *Gypsy*. New York:
    Columbia Records, 1959. Original Broadway cast album.

Suzuki, Tadashi. *The Way of Acting: The Theatre Writings of Tadashi Suzuki*.
    Trans. J. Thomas Rimer. New York: Theatre Communications
    Group, 1986.

Tait, Peta. *Performing Emotions: Gender, Bodies, Spaces in Chekhov's Drama
    and Stanislavski's Theatre*. Aldershot, UK: Ashgate, 2002.

Thompson, James. *Performance Affects: Applied Theatre and the End
    of Effect*. Basingstoke, UK, and New York: Palgrave Macmillan,
    2009.

Warner, Sara. 'Rage Slaves: The Commodification of Affect in the Five
    Lesbian Brothers' *The Secretaries*.' *Journal of Dramatic Theory and
    Critcism* 13 (2008): 21–45.

Waters, Hazel. *Racism on the Victorian Stage: Representation of Slavery and
    the Black Character*. Cambridge: Cambridge UP, 2007.

Wicker, Bruno, Christian Keysers, Jane Plailly, Jean-Pierre Royet,
    Vittorio Gallese, and Giacomo Rizzolatti. 'Both of Us Disgusted
    in My Insula: The Common Neural Basis of Seeing and Feeling
    Disgust.' *Neuron* 40 (2003): 655–64.

Zarrilli, Phillip B. *Acting (Re)considered: Theories and Practices*. New York:
    Routledge, 1995.

Zeami. *On the Art of the Nō Drama: The Major Treatises of Zeami*. Trans. J.
    Thomas Rimer and Yamazaki Masakazu. Princeton, NJ: Princeton
    UP, 1984.

index

acknowledgements

I extend my sincere thanks to Jen Harvie, who made the process of writing this book enjoyable and rewarding; to Sara Warner for stimulating and challenging conversations on theatre and feeling, and for her feedback on the text; to Amanda Clarke for her assistance in editing the text and making it sharper; to Anna Roth Trowbridge for tracking down key sources; to the three classes of 'ENGL459: Theatre and Feeling' at McGill (2007–10) who let me experiment with them; and finally to the Social Sciences and Humanities Research Council of Canada, whose Standard Research Grant programme supplied funds for research assistance and enabled teaching release when it was most needed.

To Mark, this book is affectionately dedicated.